Louise
    with love from
        Kitty & Freda.

Dee. 1942.

ST. GEORGE OR THE DRAGON

Towards a Christian Democracy

ST. GEORGE
OR THE DRAGON

Towards a Christian Democracy

by

LORD ELTON

COLLINS

48 PALL MALL LONDON

1942

THIS BOOK IS SET IN FONTANA, A NEW TYPE FACE DESIGNED
FOR THE EXCLUSIVE USE OF THE HOUSE OF COLLINS, AND
PRINTED BY THEM IN GREAT BRITAIN

First Impression	-	-	-	-	January, 1942
Second „	-	-	-	-	March, 1942
Third „	-	-	-	-	August, 1942

COLLINS CLEAR-TYPE PRESS : LONDON AND GLASGOW
COPYRIGHT

Multitudes, multitudes in the valley of decision.

The Prophet Joel.

When the scourge
Inexorable, and the torturing hour
Calls us to penance.

Milton, *Paradise Lost.*

He that wrestles with us strengthens our nerves, and sharpens our will. Our antagonist is our helper.

Burke, *Reflections on the Revolution in France.*

By this time, like one who had got out of his way by night, and travelled through a region of smooth and idle dreams, our history now arrives on the confines, where daylight and truth meet us with a clear dawn, representing to our view, though at far distance, true colours and shapes.

Milton, *History of Britain.*

CONTENTS

FOREWORD

WHO can contemplate this war without recognising that it is the supreme arbitrament of our fitness for survival, and that we have no right to hope to survive unless we are worthy to survive—and to shape the new world? And who, recognising this, can help anxiously reflecting upon our qualities, and their defects, in the light of this final and most searching test? Or, remembering that, if we survive, we must be the chief architects of the new world, has not speculated as to what sort of character our thoughts, words and deeds suggest that we might one day be ready to impose upon that other age ? This book follows more or less the pattern of such reflections as these, and in a sense, accordingly, although it is certainly concerned neither with the history of the Armistice, nor with blue prints of a New Order, it may be said to be a survey of the tragic past and the obscure future in the light of the tremendous present. Naturally it touches here and there upon matters of controversy in political, as well as other fields, but not, I hope, from the standpoint of any one Party. Some readers of the second chapter will at once write the author down an inveterate opponent of "progress," while others, if they reach the sixth, may choose to class him as a Socialist. In fact, however, there are only two permanent prejudices to which I should be ready to plead guilty, and for which the judicious reader should allow. For one thing, I believe that change, however sweeping, should have its roots in the past, and for another, I am a Christian.

I

TEST FOR SURVIVAL

§1

I AM beginning to write in the trough of the war.
No man knows what the morrow will bring. The imperial
forces are bundled helter-skelter out of Greece; the roof
of Westminster Abbey and the Commons' Chamber are
shattered; Rudolf Hess flies to Scotland—the grotesque
events succeed each other as unintelligible and as unpredictable as a nightmare. The future appears as one
vast interrogation mark. As to whether my family and
I shall be alive to-morrow, or next year, or when the war
is over, and whether, if alive, we shall, or shall not, be
bankrupt or starving or homeless it would be foolish even
to hazard a guess. Few statesmen would be willing to
prophesy how their own countries, or the world itself,
will be governed in five years' time, save those who have to
do so for the sake of propaganda. Our civilisation is in
dissolution. And yet, although we may not know certainly
what was the meaning of the war until long after the war is
over, it must have a meaning. And in a sense its meaning is
already as plain as a Panzer division. It is creating a
new world. Either the Nazis will have the making of that
new world, or we and the Americans and Russians shall.
And, once established, this new era, be it noted, may well
last, as Hitler has often boasted, for a thousand years.
For, though we are fond of saying that even Hitler cannot
hold down reluctant nations by force for ever, it is very
doubtful whether this is true. Before the development of
the bombing aeroplane and the tank, it may have been

9

true that a sufficiently determined nation was bound, sooner or later, to free itself from those who had enslaved it; for, before the development of the bombing aeroplane and the tank, sufficient rifles, combined with courage and well-organised conspiracy, could usually effect a successful revolution. And the strain on the conqueror of continuing to prevent the secret storage of rifles, the secret preparations for revolt, must sooner or later become intolerable. But you cannot secretly store bombing aeroplanes and tanks. And however passionately, even after new generations have been born to slavery, a defeated nation may continue to desire to regain its freedom, once it has been permanently deprived of its aeroplanes and tanks it must be powerless against rulers who retain an air force and a mechanised army. Whoever, therefore, has the moulding of that molten world which will emerge from the crucible of war may shape the destiny of man for an incalculable length of time. He—if the task should fall to an individual he—may well exercise upon mankind a profounder influence than any human being who has yet appeared in history. The war, in other words, is above all a supreme crisis in the eternal evolutionary struggle of nations, and governments, and ideas. One type of nation, one type of government, one system of politics and ethics and metaphysics will survive. Its rivals will disappear, like the mastodon. If, in the last great crisis of this struggle for survival, Napoleon had succeeded in establishing himself, as he so nearly did, as despot of all Europe, there would doubtless nevertheless have been further opportunities for challenging the principle of military autocracy. Even Europe, perhaps even his own Frenchmen, he could not have held down for long. And there would still have been America, beyond his reach. But this time, thanks to the power and scope of the modern war-machine, there will be no return matches. It is survival, or extinction.

§2

War, however much we may hate it, is still the supreme agent of the evolutionary process. Blind, brutal and destructive, it remains the final arbiter, the one test mankind has yet contrived of a nation's fitness to survive. Somewhere within the maniac orgy of destruction a cold scientific process is at work. It is as though, instead of a laboratory investigation with samples and test-tubes, a scientist were to need to burn down a city to find the answer to his problem. Despite all its aspirations, mankind has never yet succeeded in putting an end to war, for the simple reason that all expedients and substitutes which have so far been improvised, from the Grand Design to the League of Nations, have blandly overlooked the necessity, if war is to disappear, of providing some alternative agent of the evolutionary process. With varying degrees of short-sightedness and mental confusion, all our architects of perpetual peace have been primarily interested in stabilising the *status quo*. From first to last what interested the League of Nations, for example, was protection against the aggressor. But as often as not the aggressor represents the forces of evolution. There will never be perpetual peace until we can organise perpetual change. It is the business of an international system, such as the League aspired to be, to provide, not protection against aggression, but a substitute for it. Until that supreme problem has been solved, instead of shelved, peace can only be maintained by some power in possession of overwhelming strength, and whether it is a paramount

German Herrenvolk or an International Police Force
which exercises it, it will be seeking to stifle the most
powerful force in nature. For evolution is growth,
evolution is life. And as the crushed grass will eventually
force its tender blades through crannies in the most
titanic masonry, so at long last, even in an age which
has made the war-machine more powerful than ever
before, the inevitable forces of evolution will split the
most solid political structure, which ignores them, into
fragments. Indeed the British Commonwealth has
survived precisely because it has so conspicuously possessed
this evolutionary quality, providing within its own
elastic framework for an unparalleled degree of change.
Evolution is life, and war is still its principal agent,
selecting, by the most wasteful, yet the most decisive,
means conceivable, which nation shall survive. Not an
indispensable agent, by any means, nor yet by any means
the only agent, but nevertheless an agent of immense
potency, to which we have of late been disposed wishfully
to shut our eyes, and with which we must now fully
reckon, if we are to survive. The science of military
strategy has hitherto devoted itself far too exclusively
to studying military movement, instead of the national
organisation which made that movement possible.
To-day it must surely be plain that the total warfare of
our time is a struggle not between armies, fleets and air
forces merely, but between nations themselves, their
every quality and their every resource. In such a contest
there is no virtue, no speck of rottenness, and indeed no
idiosyncrasy in any cranny of society, which may not
have its influence upon the outcome. Almost every
important war has been won by new military inventions.
Which nation is best organised for making them? Again,
in a country in which profit is the main motive of

industry, it may be easier to get aeroplane frames manufactured than aeroplane engines, since there is a quicker
profit to be earned on the frames, whereas a country in
which industry serves the state can manufacture engines,
if it so pleases, to the complete exclusion of frames. Or
again, a nation which, in peace-time at any rate, is not
proud of its army, so that in its fiction soldiers usually
figure as Blimps or butchers, and officers do not wear
their uniforms when off duty, is less likely to attract the
best brains to soldiering than a people among whom,
however ridiculously in our eyes, there is a tradition of
cringing admiration for the military caste.

In this fantastically costly and clumsy manner, therefore,
we are now engaged in measuring ourselves, soul and
body, against the Germans. Whether we recognise it or
not, our supreme war aim, indeed our only war aim, is to
prove that Nazidom, and not ourselves, is obsolete; that
in the British Commonwealth and not in the empire of
Hitler, dwells the living germ of the age to come.

§ 3

Ought we to permit ourselves the comforting assumption that we possess one invincible ally—the retribution
which waits upon the wicked; that because Nazidom is
bad it must be beaten? Undoubtedly we have been
disposed to lay this flattering unction to our souls; and
it is probably true that in the early stages of the war the
instinctive persuasion (cherished, oddly enough, by the
most confirmed rationalists), that the invisible forces of
righteousness would somehow do most of the fighting
for us, did a good deal to deprive us of that mingled *elan*
and desperation of which, in our belated efforts to arm

13

ourselves adequately, we stood in such sore need. Now I believe that it is true that all evil is ultimately self-destructive, and that in the long run consequently right must triumph over wrong—or rather, for we are speaking of human affairs, that the better must defeat the worse. But it may be a very long run indeed. Seen in the light of eternity, a century, ten centuries for that matter, is but a moment of time. When Tennyson, in a more optimistic age, wrote that "Somehow good, Will be the final goal of ill," he was not necessarily being over-optimistic; but the important word is "final." The fundamental illusion in the once-fashionable Idea of Progress, nourished by the era of scientific discovery, was the assumption that progress, like the scientific advances of the nineteenth century, is both inevitable and more or less continuous, a process to be seen and measured within the span of each generation. But progress is neither inevitable nor continuous. Evil, it is clear, can only be defeated if there exists good to defeat it, and often in the past evil has been triumphant for generations—because there was not the good to resist it, and man needed to pass through the crucible before enough of the dross was purged away, and the good was strong enough to win another of its partial and precarious victories. The barbarous ages after the fall of Rome, the anarchy under Stephen, the wars of the Roses—our forefathers could doubtless have spared themselves all these dark nights of the spirit if only they had taken sufficient trouble; and if the good within them had been strong enough, they would assuredly have taken the trouble. But it seems that it needed those periods of desolation to spur them to the necessary effort, and it may be that, left to themselves, without either the moral energy or the grim incentives, they would have come to some more disastrous and lasting catastrophe. Man has been permitted free will, and is at liberty to make the most almighty mess of his own affairs; a mess, as often as not, which it is left to others, remote in space or time, to clear away, or put up with. Nothing in history or theology suggests that, because Nazi rule is evil, it is impossible that the world should now be plunged into a thousand years of slavery to it.

But if we must not rely upon the mere fact that Nazidom is wicked to bring retribution upon it, at any rate within our time, or the time of our children's children, may we suppose that the evil in the system must nevertheless somehow make it less efficient, and therefore less formidable in war? This is perhaps the same question, put in another way. Evil is always ultimately, but by no means always quickly, self-destructive. And modern machine-war does not allow the mills of God, which are proverbially slow, much time for grinding. A virile race of barbarians, barren of all but the military virtues, and ignorant of all arts save that of war, may speedily destroy an ancient, effete and self-indulgent civilisation, though it is not likely to survive the victory for long. Obviously, however, there are many vices which must render the nation which indulges in them less able to stand up to the searching tests of modern warfare. No country, for example, in which there is acute social, economic or political injustice, or widespread cowardice and greed, or whose civil service is incompetent or overworked, can possibly develop its full fighting strength. The total warfare of to-day makes such vast and exacting demands that no nation can conduct it successfully without possessing great qualities. But vice and virtue are strangely interwoven. One can conceive, for example, a horde of fanatical young men so devoted to, or blinded by, an ideal which fed on cruelty, perjury and paganism that for it they were ready to practise every austerity, shoulder every sacrifice and face every danger. Here would be some of the higest virtues—self-control, self-sacrifice and courage—all in servitude to the blackest evil. A nation with these contrasting qualities might prove immensely formidable in war, and, if it were victorious in war, it might be many generations before its sins eventually found it out.

§4

It would be prudent, therefore, not to underrate our opponents, wiser to assume that their vices will not do our fighting for us. Our business is to consider our own quality. The enemy may be evil, and history may suggest that in the long run what we call good will be too much for what we call evil, that good is survival and that evil is self-destruction; yet what right have we to assume that the mysterious title to survival is embodied in ourselves? Is it not possible, after all, to champion virtue without possessing it, to defend the ultimate moral standards without living up to them, to fight for democracy without practising it, to risk our lives for Christendom without being Christians? Such are some of the first questions we have to put to ourselves at a time such as this. They will lead us to many others. Long ago men believed that the supreme tasks, such as the Crusades or the quest of the Grail, demanded of those who undertook them not only, perhaps not so much, a certain quality of life in the past, as a progressive effort of self-discipline in the present. It was not so much the crusader who made the crusade as the crusade which made the crusader. To win your victory you had, sooner or later, to earn it. Your enemy might be a brute, a tyrant and a pagan, but victory would not drop into your lap, unless, or until, you yourself were decent, just and Christian. It was a belief which can find considerable support in history, not to speak of theology. The school of adversity has not seldom proved a nursery of the sterner virtues. And the doctrine of regeneration through suffering has been cherished in all ages by the most spiritually advanced among mankind. For us, therefore, the supreme purpose and meaning of this war must be that we are offered an opportunity of becoming worthy of victory in it.

Perhaps the use of the word purpose needs some apology. And yet almost everybody feels instinctively that the life of a man, and the life of man, is not mere sound and fury, signifying nothing. Indeed some of those who would be the first to deride the ancient notion of a benign supernatural overruling of human history have often, like Thomas Hardy or Professor A. E. Housman, seemed among the readiest to believe in a supernatural overruling, provided only that it be malignant. It is by no means only theists who have claimed that a purpose can be precariously distinguished beneath the tides of human affairs, a purpose which in the great crises of history seems sometimes for a moment to stand forth unmistakable. Whatever that purpose may be, however, it is most certainly not the purpose as to which Victorian Liberalism was so proudly positive. It is not their "Progress." Already it is difficult to believe that this strange and long-lived illusion actually flourished until the day before yesterday, and indeed that the jargon of the cult still lingers on, so that people will even now claim to be "progressive," with the same faintly self-righteous unction with which a Roundhead might have announced that he belonged to the godly party. And yet for many, perhaps for most, of the strongest intellects of the last hundred and fifty years the notion that on stepping-stones of his dead selves man marches inevitably towards perfection was a burning faith, as often as not the nearest that they came to a religion. In his preface to the *Origin of Species* the great Darwin shows himself as devout and credulous a believer in perfectibility as Dr. Joseph Priestley, the eighteenth-century Nonconformist controversialist. And by the end of the nineteenth century, after a hundred years of mechanical inventions, the belief that some apocalyptic Dawn was close at hand was almost a commonplace. "Progress is not an accident," wrote Herbert Spencer, "but a necessity. What we call evil and immorality must disappear. It is certain that man must become perfect." Swinburne's symbolically named *Songs before Sunrise* was intended as a salute to the golden age to be—atheist, republican and sexually promiscuous. Born in 1892, when the religion of Progress was at its zenith, a soldier in 1914, a parent in 1939, I have lived long enough to see its fruits. No, if there is a purpose in the lives of men, or in the life of mankind, it is assuredly not this brand of Progress. We certainly do not rise automatically upon the stepping-stones of our dead selves. On the contrary, so far from sin and error declining as truth and virtue increase, the evil grows along with the good. At every stage of history man is offered the same eternal choice between the two. Always he can go back or go forward, build or destroy. As his powers for good increase, so do his powers for evil. At every crisis in history he must choose, and always he is free to choose disastrously. That is the meaning of every crisis in history; it is a choice. The fortieth century will be as free as the twentieth to revert to the law of the jungle, or the morals of the farmyard, and call it Progress. Good and evil grow together. The servants of the householder, it may be recalled, inquired whether they should gather up the tares; and he answered, No; *let both grow together till the harvest.* Let both grow together to the harvest; it could not be better put.

And so all history, and indeed all life, is a crisis. For crisis is a Greek word, signifying judgment, or decision. And the choices which, whether we like it or not, we are for ever making are both decisions and judgments. We choose what to do or say or think, and, in choosing, pass judgment on ourselves also. All history is a crisis, and its greatest moments are those in which the greatest decisions must be made. For the inevitable antinomy is always there. Great good cannot be achieved unless great evil be avoided. For good does not just happen, as the cult of Progress often appeared to assume. Good is necessarily a victory over evil. And this is why some of the most memorable advances of humanity have been recorded at the very moment when it appeared to stand upon the verge of the abyss, so that men have often gone forward from some tremendous cross-roads, at which they seemed upon the point of turning aside to chaos and frustration. Such a moment is upon us now. This war, like its grim and protracted preliminaries, is indeed, as the popular Press has been only too fond of reminding us, a crisis. It is the moment of judgment and decision; a supreme opportunity of evil, but also a supreme opportunity of good. We shall not achieve victory unless we become worthy of it, but if we do become worthy of it we shall achieve more than victory. For this time it cannot be merely a question of beating off the challenge of Prussian militarism. This time we cannot help ourselves; the world must go far back or far forward. And this is why our war aim

cannot now be this reform or that, not "social justice" or
the restoration of Czechoslovakia or a new paper League
of Nations, but rather to prove that it is tyranny which is
obsolete, and not the British Commonwealth.

§5

This is the justification of all the recent talk about a
New Social Order. That sudden fashion was curiously
significant. It was by no means only mere escapism,
although of course, if you are living in a heavily bombed
area, it is tempting to let your thoughts dwell upon the
New Jerusalem. The New Social Orderers would probably
have accounted for their enthusiasm in various ways.
Some would have said that a nation which can devote so
much money, so much energy and so much valour to
Armageddon must not shirk the moral and economic
effort required to polish off the chief outstanding social
problems after the war. Others might have said that so
much anarchy and destruction would be too hideous to
contemplate, if they could not believe that somehow
good was to come out of it. Others, doubtless, believed
that the secret of Progress had long since been disclosed
to them, and that in the stress of war the barriers which
had hitherto baffled them would go down. But, however
they expressed themselves, all were probably dimly aware
that the war is a supreme test of fitness for survival, a
contest, first and foremost, to decide who shall shape the
future, and that if we are to survive we cannot afford
merely to defend the past. And it is probable that they
exaggerated the consequent obligation on themselves to
plan the future largely because they were most of them
unfortunately so blind to the nature and achievements of

the British Commonwealth of nations, which is in itself at once a title to survival, and a programme for the future, of the first magnitude, with which, for novelty and promise, Hitler's New Order cannot begin to compare. Another somewhat less creditable motive of the cult of paper constitutions may have been that some of the planners counted on solving all the problems of the new world by the speedy enforcement of systems which they, and others, have been persistently advocating, and the electorate as persistently rejecting, for the last fifty years. They proposed in fact to indulge in a peculiar form of war profiteering, by using Armageddon as a sort of smoke-screen for the advance of their own favourite theories. All such enthusiasts ignore the fact that the new age will infallibly be a *new* age. It will be firmly rooted, let us hope, in our history, it will contain the familiar landmarks; but its characteristic problems will be new problems, and will only be disposed of by new solutions. It is not only the institutions which planners of the future are most apt to deride which may find themselves out of date—not only Conservatism or the bench of Bishops or the *Times*. Communism and surrealism and nudism, and a score of other Isms, will find themselves equally outmoded, equally tainted by the past —and in all probability indeed far more completely outmoded, since they will "date" irremediably, being redolent of one transient phase in that immediate past, which is always remotest from present sympathy, and since they are not, like more ancient institutions, the ever-changing product of the idiosyncrasies of many generations. It is certain at any rate that what is needed now is not what New Social Orderers have on the whole been disposed to offer us—a paper constitution from the bureau or the lecture-room, an amalgam of the *a priori*

plans of experts and cranks. For one thing, this country
has never cared much for *a priori* plans or paper constitutions, and has preferred to proceed empirically from
problem to problem, tackling them successively by the
compass-bearing, so to speak, of a long-descended instinct
for self-government, and that broad consensus as to
the general line of advance which has almost always
underlain the superficial Party controversies. Nor has
this resulted, as might have been expected, in a mere
patchwork of haphazard improvisation. In its instinctive
reaction to crisis a society such as this, mellowed by
centuries of organic growth, can draw upon profounder
sources of instinctive wisdom than any planning committee of experts. The foundations of the New Order
have been laid already, amid the bombs and the evacuations and in the devastated streets. For in a society such
as ours, which has grown instead of being manufactured,
the future lies always within the womb of the present,
and to-day most of the processes of growth have been
immensely accelerated by the stress of war. Paper constitutions are superfluous; the building of the new
society has begun. This does not mean, of course, that
there should be no planning, or that New Jerusalems
can be built without taking thought for the morrow, by
mere empiricism and instinct. What it does mean is that
the empirical and the instinctive have always counted for
much more in our political processes than in those of
other countries, and for very much more than is ever
allowed for by the ideologue. Also that the "planner,"
accordingly, has to go to work within that framework
with which empiricism and instinct will have already
presented him. And to-day, when life is one vast complex
of unprecedented but urgent problems, it is natural that
empiricism and instinct should be building more of the

framework, and building it quicker, than ever before. In relation to the future our task is therefore, up to a point, to foresee, and only beyond that point, to will.

For we stand between two ages. The war is the great crucible in which we must qualify to shape the future by sloughing the shortcomings of the past. By the fiery light of the present, therefore, it is our business first to test our past, and then both to foresee, and to will, the future.

II

THE ASSAULT UPON MORALE

§1

IT is impossible, of course, to divide the life or character of a nation into watertight compartments; each inter-penetrates the others; social problems affect administrative organisation, economic structure reacts upon art. And of all the aspects from which a nation can be viewed, after its spiritual faith its moral standards go furthest to condition the whole of the rest of its life, and are therefore perhaps the hardest to isolate. All the same, they are, for that very reason, in the highest degree symptomatic. And on war they have a particular and vital bearing. In war-time morale is all; and morale is only morals viewed from a special angle and disguised by a slight change of spelling—almost as if we felt it safer to face the supreme test with a new set of qualities altogether, in place of the somewhat ramshackle outfit inherited from peace-time. Possibly for the same reason we have a way, in war-time at any rate, of treating the military virtues as though they were peculiar and specialised qualities, only needed, or to be admired, in soldiers. And yet the military virtues are the most fundamental and familiar of all virtues. They are not militarism; militarism perverts them to its own use. They are the basis of civilisation itself—loyalty, courage, endurance, discipline. Indeed, if it comes to that, though they are not the only Christian virtues—are there not also faith, hope and charity?—they are very close to the core of the Christian religion, for they can all be reduced to a single quality—unselfishness. In surveying first the qualities which make for moral stamina in warfare, and what some of our intellectual leaders have been doing for them during the last twenty years, I do not wish to be understood to suppose that that is the supreme test of morals as well as of morale. All the same, here as elsewhere war is the test of our fitness to survive, it is in this crucible that our qualities are being assayed, and the virtues required in warfare are so fundamental that those who seek to undermine them are not merely reducing our ability to fight, but poisoning the soul of the nation. Nevertheless this chapter, which will seem annoyingly controversial, I am afraid, to some, surveys only a portion of the field. Beyond and beneath the attack upon the military virtues lay a century of soft and greedy materialism, and the surrender of the Christian philosophy. To these profounder and spiritual maladies I shall come later, and by degrees. Seen in due perspective, the movements which I am now recalling were only perhaps the froth and surface clamour of those deeper currents. Nevertheless they concern the qualities first tested by modern war; they are recent, and noisy, and still obsess many imaginations; and it is as well to weigh their significance at once, and, having done so, to forget them.

§2

Loyalty, courage, endurance, discipline; without these, in abundant measure, we certainly shall not survive the present ordeal. Loyalty, courage, endurance, discipline, not in a select warrior caste only, not in great armies of trained soldiers, but in the entire mass of ordinary citizens. At first sight it is certainly a tall order. And yet a democrat at least should not be sceptical about the possibility of the masses displaying these virtues; for the essence of democracy is faith in the virtue of the ordinary man. The ruler, the wealthy, the intellectuals, all these may be corrupted, by power, by luxury or by a nimblé, but blinkered, intelligence. But the very simplicity of the common man may enable him to preserve the simple virtues. "It is not the man of politics, or the man of letters," wrote Rabindranath Tagore, "but the simple man whose faith is living; let us believe in his instinct; let his expectation guide us to our wealth." It was this manifest superiority, in the essential virtues, of most of the simple and obscure to most of their pastors and masters which led Rousseau to denounce civilisation as corruption, and proclaim the virtues of the natural man; as it may have prompted Christ to thank the Almighty for concealing certain truths from the wise and prudent and revealing them unto babes. It is a contrast always worth remembering, since common humanity is seldom vocal, and as we turn the pages of history it is usually to the powerful, the wealthy or the intellectual— and in particular to the latter—that we are listening; but it is particularly worth remembering when we consider our own record in respect of these same military virtues. For it does not follow that, where the vocal minority affects to despise the military virtues, the non-vocal majority has ceased to practise them. And yet the fact remains that it is the vocal minority which makes history. Nations rot from the top downwards. While Pétain despaired and Laval double-crossed, it may be that the French peasants, and even most of the French workmen, remained as loyal and hardy as their forebears. In spite of which France fell.

§3

The attitude of our spokesmen at least towards the fundamental military virtues has followed a well-marked curve over the last quarter of a century. During the last war, needless to say, no praise was too high for those who displayed them. Once again, for a brief while, they had come into their own. For although opinions may differ as to whether the military virtues can safely be dispensed with in peace-time, nobody, as far as I know, has yet suggested that war can be successfully waged without loyalty, courage, endurance and discipline. During the last war, accordingly, while the ruler was often suspect, the wealthy scorned and the intellectuals effaced, the common man in the trenches, the Poor Bloody Infantry, was for once the object of universal admiration. War had stripped life for the time being down to the hard core of reality, and unselfish service counted for more than successful profiteering, and a stout heart for more than an agile pen. This reversal of customary values did not long outlast the war which was responsible for it. For the war itself, to which the young had dedicated themselves with such exalted hopes in 1914, and soon afterwards the fighting men themselves, passed under a cloud. In 1918 it

27

was a little too soon for those who for four years had
stood critically and restively aside from the struggle—
Above the Conflict as Romain Rolland somewhat in-
genuously put it—to deride the soldierly virtues under
whose temporary prestige they had chafed; but Lytton
Strachey's *Eminent Victorians*, the first important manifesto of the reaction, and a book of immense literary
influence, did the next best thing, by discreetly guying
various historical personages whom the Victorians had
admired for courage, endurance or achievement. These
men and women, so ran the thesis, were not heroes and
heroines; they were not even villains; like every one else
of whom the man in the street has made a hero, they were
only mildly ridiculous. It was a tired, timid, recluse's
book, which a perplexed and exhausted public hailed as a
welcome return from the crudities of war to the suaver
standards of civilisation, but which for some of those who
were conscious of not having played their part in the
struggle was a foretaste of the moral revolution which
would restore the man of words to his customary
prominence, and the man of deeds to his proper obscurity.
It proved to be the forerunner of a prolific literature,
whose ideal, if it can be said to have possessed an ideal,
was a critical detachment from the passions and illusions
of humanity, a detachment, in other words, from life
itself; a literature for which, outside the sciences, all
achievement, like the fundamental human virtues on
which achievement depends, was faintly "bogus;" a
literature which could titter at almost anything and
could admire almost nothing; a literature, in brief,
founded upon fatigue, disillusionment and an inferiority
complex. After Strachey's polished innuendoes, the
inevitable frontal attack upon the accepted values of
war-time developed more slowly; but well before the

Armistice, Siegfried Sassoon's passionate *Counter Attack*, while full of praise and pity for front-line soldiers, showed little respect for "the smugfaced crowds" who cheered them, and none at all for the war which they were fighting. And soon after the return of peace, C. E. Montagu, who had also been a fighting man, produced, in *Disenchantment*, a reasoned exposure of the shabbier undertones of a war which had begun with idealism and ended in disillusionment. Though Montagu obviously had a proper respect for the soldierly qualities, with which indeed he was himself conspicuously endowed, it was part of his theme that the fighting man also degenerated during the long process of disenchantment, so that by the last year of war the cynic, the shirker and the self-seeker were more conspicuous than the self-devoted patriots of the early months. Another year or two, and the last inhibitions were overcome; the full revulsion, not only against the war but against the men who fought it, had set in. The shell-shocked, the embusqués, and the thorough-going pacifists were free to give tongue again. In defeated and despairing Germany the fashion was already at its height, and two German novels, translated as *All Quiet on the Western Front* and *The Case of Sergeant Grischa*, served as incentive to our own iconoclasts. There was an even readier market for such wares in Britain. For Germany had at least been defeated. There was the incentive of recovery and revenge, for one thing. Moreover there was not the same disillusionment; nobody, after all, had expected defeat to be pleasant. But Britain had been victorious. Here there was nothing left to strive for; the ripe fruits of victory should have fallen into our lap; had we not been taught to expect a land fit for heroes, and a world safe for democracy? That the only certain consequence of victory was negative

—not to have been destroyed—that this in itself was a
tremendous consequence, and that we might perhaps not
have earned any other, all this nobody had as yet taught
us. For the eagerly devoured war fiction of the next
few years the war was almost always a pointless and
ignoble shambles—"this immense crop of murders"—
and the successful soldier usually brutal, dull or drunken.
The heroes of the characteristic war novel were apt to be
hypersensitive young persons whose spiritual revolt was
represented as much more creditable than the placid
discipline of their companions. The motive of the
authors may often have been to make sure that the world
did not too readily forget the horrors of war, and there
is the natural reaction against the more sentimental
patriotism of war-time to be taken into account, but it is
difficult to resist the impression that they were too
frequently only dramatising their own frustration, or
failure, as soldiers, or their own refusal to serve; there
was a good deal of inferiority complex latent in the
"war is Hell" best-sellers. Certainly the collective impression which they combined to present of the four
years' struggle proved highly perplexing to most of those
who had shared in the experiences which they portrayed.
Art, no doubt, is always subjective, but here nature seemed
to have been viewed through an exceptionally distorting
medium. One was reminded of some familiar countryside transformed in a Cubist landscape, so difficult was it,
as one searched the membership of one's own branch of
the British Legion, or one's memory of one's own
comrades in arms, to encounter even one per cent of the
star-crossed and neurotic warriors who populated the
war fiction of these years so abundantly. Meanwhile the
young, who had missed the war, and felt themselves
excluded from a great experience, began to join the timid

or weakly, who had evaded it, in maintaining this triple fashion, of belittling the normal soldier and the normal soldier's virtues, of luxuriating in the horrors of war, and of writing down the consequences of victory. It was of this powerful tendency that G. K. Chesterton was thinking when he wrote: "I am all the more anxious to avert another war now that I know that my friends and brethren are henceforth doomed to suffer twice for the sin of patriotism; to be destroyed by their enemies and despised by their countrymen." The pacifists, too, many of them genuine and courageous idealists, not un-naturally supported this more equivocal reaction against the fighting men, and indeed went far to make it respect-able. The reaction was fairly launched.

A considerable majority of the writers who ex-ercised the most obvious influence on the post-war generation were men, or women, more or less consciously in revolt against the war of 1914-1918, the men who fought it and the qualities which they had displayed.

The soldiers, on the other hand, who had returned from the trenches enriched and not frustrated remained on the whole unvocal. For of those who might have presented the war in fuller perspective—as a tragedy indeed, but not a meaningless and squalid tragedy merely; as a catastrophe on the grand scale, out of which good on the grand scale might nevertheless be wrested—of those too few had returned. They might have taught the new generation the ancient lesson that suffering, accepted and understood, can enrich men with new wisdom and strength.

This was a lesson, it is true, which countless inconspic-uous lives were there to illustrate, but which found little acceptance among the vocal. And too few of the men who might have taught it had survived the war. All wars inevitably kill off the fittest, for inevitably the fittest are sent first to the posts of danger; but no war as yet can have destroyed so high a proportion of the moral élite as did the war of 1914 to 1918, in Britain. In those first, worst years, before we had brought ourselves to face conscription, hecatombs of the courageous and unselfish selected themselves automatically for destruction. Those who were physically or morally more poorly qualified, who for one reason or another preferred to control margarine, or to drive ambulances behind the lines, or who were too conscientious to fight at all, these survived, out of all normal proportion—to set the fashions of the post-war age.

§ 4

This triple fashion, first conspicuous in the early war fiction, lingered on until all traditions were temporarily overwhelmed by the coming of a new war. As with those intellectuals who had surveyed the last war from the wings, or whose unsatisfactory part in it had saddled them for life with a subconscious self-contempt, the soldier remained, on the whole, a target of faintly patronising derision. As the young man, conscious of his own inexperience, secretly reassures himself by an all-embracing irreverence towards his elders, so perhaps some of these writers were unconsciously compensating themselves for lack of stamina or courage by fostering the convention that all soldiers have wooden heads, and that patriotism is out of date. For courage is the basic virtue, and however intelligent, popular or wealthy he may be, a man will always feel secretly inferior to one whom he knows to be more courageous than himself, and will usually be tempted, in consequence, to still his secret misgivings by emphasising in public the superiority of intelligence or wealth or popularity to courage.

It was only natural that when a brilliant popular cartoonist required a sort of ventriloquist's dummy to symbolise dull wits and old-fashioned obscurantism he should have selected a soldier, the now celebrated Colonel Blimp. This popular figure did not appear until the 'thirties, when a National Government was once again reviving ancient memories by sounding, if more than half apologetically, a muted note of patriotism. But his prototype had frequently figured in Low's work. Thus in a cartoon of December, 1929, protesting against an apparent decline in the still-flourishing fashion of anti-war, and anti-patriotic fiction, and the consequent prospect that "the professional patriots, romantic hero-worshippers . . . and incurable halfwits" may "again raise their heads," the Colonel's twin, though not yet labelled Blimp, hobbles, gouty and ferocious, in the front rank of a motley party of Generals, girl typists and ex-servicemen, displaying placards such as "Our fellows were all pure—not like the rude enemy you read of," and headed by a braying ass hung with war medals. It was characteristic of this era that the cartoons should have appeared in a newspaper owned by a Conservative, and that the Conservatives themselves were too timid and unimaginative to evolve a Left-Wing counterpart to Colonel Blimp. For anti-nationalism and aversion for everything military were items in a whole complex of opinions, an ideology in fact, which now reigned supreme, and in politics was associated with the Left. In varying degrees all the intelligent weeklies professed these views, for it was assumed that among the intelligent there was no public for any other. And even in ostensibly Conservative newspapers with large circulations the literary columns at least had been unostentatiously surrendered to those who subscribed to the prevalent conventions, and nobody thought it odd that for years the chief fiction reviewer on the Conservative *Observer* should have been a lifelong Socialist. One effect of this curious detachment, or timidity, among Conservative editors and proprietors was naturally to instil anti-Conservative opinion all but ubiquitously among the literary and intelligent, for whatever his natural prejudices might be, the ambitious young writer soon realised that he must on no account be suspected of respect for tradition if he wished for serious attention from reviewers, even in the Conservative Press. And so he usually either abandoned a literary career altogether, or else, since your modern ideology is a rigidly coherent system, his views not only on unemployment or the League of Nations, but on art, soldiers, history, morals, and many other matters apparently remote from Parliamentary controversy, soon assumed the fashionable hue.

And yet any one who will take the trouble to look back over the opinions invented for the egregious Blimp by his distinguished creator, will be surprised to discover how often, even so, it is not Low but Blimp who was right.

Not long ago the apoplectic Colonel, arrayed in his simple panoply of Turkish bath-towel, could rouse derisive laughter among the intelligent with such characteristic aphorisms as "Gad, Sir, Winston is right, we must have more armaments" (May, 1934); "Be prepared with plenty of armaments and then there will be peace" (May, 1935); "We must have conscription if Liberty is to survive" (1935); "Gad, Sir, Mr. Baldwin is right. To ensure peace we must have plenty of airplanes" (November, 1933)—an interesting commentary, this last, upon those apostles of peace who once jeered at Blimp and Mr. Baldwin for wanting aeroplanes, and now jeer at them for not having wanted them enough. In the last resort Blimp, after all, represented (to quote Mr. Arnold Lunn) "what was left in England of that feudal and aristocratic tradition which we were glad enough to make use of in time of war."

To-day Blimp is in the Home Guard, and his sons in the Air Force, while of those who derided him most eloquently some are in the United States, and others (as Professor J. M. Keynes observed in the *New Statesman*, in October, 1939) "who were the loudest in demanding that Nazi aggression should be resisted at all costs, when it comes to a show-down, scarce four weeks have passed before they remember that they are pacifists, and write defeatist letters to your columns, leaving the defence of freedom and of civilisation to Colonel Blimp and the old school tie, for whom three cheers."

Professor Keynes was right to associate the farcical symbol of the army with the farcical symbol of the public school, for both, in a sense, are relics of that earlier, feudal tradition which chose its leaders not among writers and talkers, but among those who lead their men into battle. "The monied men, merchants, principal tradesmen and men of letters (hitherto thought generally the peaceable and even timid part of society) are the chief actors," wrote Burke, "in the French Revolution." [1] And in a sense the key to the history of the century which followed is the successful, and indeed inevitable, transference of power from what may be called the officer class to Burke's "peaceable and

---

[1] I owe this quotation as well as some suggestive comments on Colonel Blimp to Mr. Arnold Lunn's *Come What May*.

even timid part of society." The obloquy of Colonel Blimp accordingly has its roots in powerful and respectable historical forces. A psychologist, however, could probably distinguish a dozen or so of contributory factors in the cult of this particular scapegoat. The traditional unpopularity of the Army, except in time of war, an unpopularity which had even induced the Iron Duke to take steps to ensure that henceforth, save when duty made it unavoidable, his officers should not show themselves in uniform in public; hatred of German militarism; fear of another war; dreams of permanent, universal peace—all these must have played their part.

The fact remains that essentially Blimp was the eternal dugout (or at least that highly choleric and obtuse individual in the almost legendary dimensions which he had lately assumed in the pages of fiction; in real life it is possible to be acquainted with a pretty considerable number of Colonels without being able to recall a single Blimp). He was a *revenant* from the last war. And by now the prejudices of the reaction against the last war, and the men who fought it, had sunk so deep into the collective mentality of the British intelligentsia, that they had passed out of the field of reason into that of the emotions, and the critical faculty of many writers who found themselves discussing events, ideas, or persons associated with the war was almost completely suspended.

Writing in the *Spectator*, in March, 1941, Miss Rose Macaulay, a novelist who made her first success with *Potterism*, a novel which satirised loose, emotional thinking in war-time, expressed scepticism as to the suggestion that a large proportion of the potential leaders of the post-war generation had fallen in the last war, since "it has been lately pointed out in this paper how small a percentage of our fighting forces in the last war were

killed." She was almost certainly thinking of a comment
on the fact that military casualties in the *present* war had,
so far, been slight; but the inadvertent transference of
the derogatory piece of information came only too
naturally. In the reaction of a quarter of a century, most
of the adulation showered on the fighting men, while
their services were still needed, had been forgotten, or
unsaid, by a softer generation; and now what might
have been thought to be their one indisputable achievement was to be denied: it was even beginning to be
believed that not many of them had been killed.[1]

§ 5

We thus embarked upon a new war handicapped by
twenty years of propaganda against the virtues needed to
win it. It soon became an assumption of pacifist propaganda that the impulse to serve one's country in arms was
bloodthirsty and uncivilised. "The ancient rhetoric of
dying for one's country covers the real purpose of warriors
in killing for one's country," wrote Mr. Delisle Burns.
Havelock Ellis, discovering with horror that Oxford
University, in 1931, possessed an inconspicuous O.T.C.,
described the University, in the *New Statesman*, as "a
centre for the destruction of civilisation." Mr. Beverly
Nichols, in a popular work of pacifist propaganda,
Cry Havoc, blamed literature for presenting everyday life
in too warlike a guise. Nor has the new war altogether
put an end to this propaganda. In the latest attack on the
public schools, *Barbarians & Philistines* by Mr. T. C.
Worsley, published after twelve months of fighting,

[1] The dead in the forces of the British Empire in the last war numbered
1,104,890.

37

fighting which included the beating off of the Luftwaffe by the pilots of the R.A.F., the author includes in his comprehensive indictment of public school obscurantism the damning charge that public schoolboys "tend to admire especially the military virtues, toughness, courage and endurance," magisterially denouncing the "self-conscious deification" in the public schools "of the virtues, loyalty, courage and endurance."

In so far as the campaign of detraction was not directed against the fundamental qualities of all fighting men, the Army inevitably became its principal target. One can hardly imagine an Admiral, still less a Wing Commander, Blimp. There are historical reasons why the Army has never been so popular, or so generously financed, as the Navy. It may be, too, that it has always had less intelligent and imaginative leadership. But there is a vicious circle here. You do not encourage able young men to enter the Army by persuading them to believe that a soldier must be dull and brutal, to make a success of his degrading butcher's trade. It is not a coincidence that, whereas the British Navy and Air Force were probably in most ways technically in advance of the enemy's, the Army's whole conception of land warfare was a generation behind that of the Germans.

The almost hysterical emphasis on the horror of war, which was the most obvious characteristic of the first reaction, survived, like the revolt against the military virtues, pervasively in every domain of literature and art. It had, of course, its merits. It was both natural and proper to resolve that if our children embarked upon another war it should at any rate not be because they did not realise that another war would be both extremely destructive and extremely unpleasant. But this does not account for the mounting note of hysteria, so often to be detected in the denunciation of war by those who had evaded, or lost their nerve in it. It has to be remembered that the characteristic spiritual background, the "mental climate," of the whole post-war reaction was an agnostic materialism. And materialism is *soft*. For the materialist, pain and death have a greater importance than any species of transcendental religion has ever allowed to them. Criticism of the literary merchants of horror, for there was some criticism, did not of course imply that the critics, like the Nazis, regarded war as man's natural occupation, at worst a blessing in disguise. They probably thought of war pretty much as they thought of disease, which a wise man dreads and seeks to avert, but does not gloat over.

§ 6

From the first it was naturally an axiom with the post-war reaction that the war had been purposeless. A vast outpouring of blood and treasure, and behold a world not magically cured of all its ill for ever, rather a world reeling headlong towards catastrophe. "The only victory that had resulted was in fact the victory of death over life, of stupidity over intelligence, of hatred over humanity." [1] Even a decade later, after so many more wasted opportunities, and from the midst of another German world war, the shallowness of that view is still apparent. Two consequences of victory were possible, one was achieved. The householder repelled the burglar. A good deal of his property was destroyed in the course of the struggle, and he sustained a number of painful wounds; but he repelled the burglar. Neither the

[1] Richard Aldington, *Roads to Glory*.

British, nor the democratic, way of life was extinguished by Prussian militarism. That alone was a tremendous result—negative, but tremendous. Unfortunately, after repelling the burglar we did not achieve the secondary and positive consequence which might have followed victory. We did not put an end to burglary. The chance was there, but we did not take it. We had not, it appeared, become fully worthy of victory, and suddenly, perplexingly, it slipped from our despairing clutches. The complete, the winged Victory, glimpsed for a moment in November, 1918, had eluded us. That does not, however, render purposeless the sacrifice of the million dead who, though they could not save themselves, did assuredly save us—from Prussia. That we who survived proved not sufficiently worthy of their victory to carry it one stage further, to the plane of the positive, this was not their fault. Much had been achieved; only, in these epochal struggles it is all or, sooner or later, nothing. This time we shall not even win the negative victory, the victory over Prussia, unless we have become worthy of the positive victory, the victory over ourselves. From the long welter of the cockpit has sooner or later to emerge a survivor fit to shape a new age. This time we must not hope to win the first victory, the victory which is survival, unless and until we are fit to win the second, the victory which is creative leadership. For this war is not merely a mortal combat, it is the great school of adversity, in which, if we are not for ever learning as we fight, we are doomed.

§ 7

This widely pervasive attitude to the soldierly virtues, to soldiers, to war and to victory, legacy of the pre-dominance in the first post-war years of those who were in revolt against the war, represented, obviously enough, a deep vein of *softness* in our literature. This was certainly not a tradition to inspire men either to dare or to endure. And if it be objected that this is only another way of saying that its high priests and apostles were highly civilised persons, in praiseworthy revolt against brutality and war, the answer, it is to be feared, must be that this was not a literature, or a tradition, to inspire to any positive achievement of any kind whatever. It was the literature of the titter, the yawn or the shrug of the shoulders. No incentive there to endeavour, in either peace or war. " Punctuality, regularity, discipline, industry are a set of slave virtues," wrote Mr. G. D. H. Cole. For most of these writers there was little hope or promise in the world of common men, but chiefly folly and despair; and the artists were apt to turn their backs upon it, retiring into the ivory castle of an esotericism which refused to address ordinary humanity, and which reached its logical conclusion in the strange writings of Miss Gertrude Stein, an authoress who achieved a considerable reputation by the apparently simple expedient of publishing what were often quite meaningless successions of words. (" Rules are not what are not sometimes and always with feathers and parallelograms are longer and not warmer when exceptions are there. A cucumber can be its own father if wanted and not wanted and not not wanted so a cucumber can be its own father if fathers are wanted and not wanted and a father can be its own cucumber if feathers are wanted and not exceptions," and so on and so on; it was much admired by the advanced.) The work of Miss Stein, or James Joyce's *Three Tales of Shem and Shaun*, in which no single sentence is intelligible, were only extreme examples of what was a general tendency in serious literature. It had become a sort of code-writing for a few thousand initiates. The fundamental cowardice of a literary movement which ignored, because it despaired of, the man in the street, found its counterpart in art. Imitations of negro sculpture, engineering diagrams, drawings which suggested the scribbling of children or lunatics, patterns framed upon chance blots or the natural shape of stones, all these followed each other with bewildering rapidity. The characteristic cults of Abstract, and Surrealist, painting were fatally divorced from humanity, and seemed to make no attempt to reflect, or comment on, the life of their own time. It was usually possible to examine an exhibition of the work of these schools without discovering, if one had not already known, whether they were products of England or Thibet, of the twentieth, or twelfth, centuries. It is quite new, this notion that "good" art or "good" literature must be "difficult." Most of the great writers of the past were best-sellers, deliberately purveying popular entertainment. Shakespeare, Scott, Dickens, Byron, Ovid, Vergil, Fielding, Euripides, Malory, Homer, Molière—the list would be almost endless. They wrote to entertain their adult contemporaries in general, and their huge publics enjoyed them naturally and unselfconsciously, with no notion of superiority in possessing the industry or the intelligence to understand something from which ordinary folk were excluded.

To quote Mr. C. S. Lewis:

"I foresee the growth of a new race of readers and critics to whom, from the very outset, good literature will be an accomplishment rather than a delight, and who will always feel, beneath the acquired taste, the backward tug of something else which they feel merit in resisting. Such people will not be content to say that some books are bad or not very good; they will make a special class of 'lowbrow' art which is to be vilified, mocked, quarantined, and sometimes (when they are sick or tired) enjoyed. They will be sure that what is popular must always be bad, thus assuming that human taste is *naturally* wrong, that it needs not only improvement and development but veritable conversion. . . . Their 'good' taste will have been acquired by the sweat of their brows and they will hold it with uneasy intensity. As they will be contemptuous of popular books, so they will be naïvely tolerant of dullness and obscurity in any quack or sloven who comes before them with lofty pretensions; *all* literature having been as hard to them as that, as much an acquired taste, they will not see the difference. They will be angry with a true lover of literature who does not take pains to unravel the latest poetical puzzle, and call him a *dilettante*. Having obtained the freedom of Parnassus at a great price, they will be unable to endure the nonchalance of those who were freeborn."[1]

[1] *Rehabilitations*, 114. See the whole admirable essay on "High and Low Brows."

§ 8

Courage, loyalty, discipline, endurance. Did the sustained campaign conducted by the few against the tough, fundamental virtues, on which not only resistance in war, but civilisation itself, depends, actually affect their practice among the many? It has to be remembered that the special hostility focused on the qualities associated with war was only one element in a wider offensive against traditional morals as a whole, an offensive which, though its range and impetus increased enormously during the last two decades, was deeply rooted in nineteenth-century rationalism. There lies beside me at the moment a bookseller's catalogue commending what it describes as the "progressive, enlightened moral paganism" of Swinburne's poetry. For it was one of the odder illusions of the rationalist cult to hail as one aspect of "progress" the despairing relapse to the standards of the jungle and the farm. Here was a spreading streak of softness, on which the post-war reaction was only too ready to seize. For civilisation is self-discipline, and its advance is measured by man's gradual mastery of his more savage instincts. The easy practice of "Do as you please," whether it meant predatory lawlessness or sexual promiscuity, had slowly to be replaced, as man climbed out of the dark ages, by a more exacting code. But the ascent has been both painful and intermittent; in society at its most civilised there have always been enclaves of anti-social practice, in which "Do as you please" has been openly practised, if not publicly preached; and in phases of laxity and regression the dark aboriginal instincts may overflow their Abbeys of Thélème, and parade as a novel and nation-wide cult, with its brass-band

44

of accommodating publicists duly in attendance. Such a moment recurred when the sudden Armistice had relaxed the intolerable tensions of four years of war. A discreet reflection of the promiscuity and perversion which were fashionable in the post-war years can be traced by the curious investigator in the Press of that time. A more accessible and stylised picture may be found in the early novels of Mr. Aldous Huxley. It will be noted, however, that this author at least was not under the illusion that the primitive lusts are a novel form of civilised enlightenment—indeed there are few more terrifying pictures of the miseries of hedonism than the study of Spandrell in *Point Counterpoint*. For fiction in general, however, the convention was that, whatever heroic qualities were permitted the hero or heroine, and these were not many, the overcoming of lust must on no account be among them. In this way fiction made its own contribution to the sins of the world, and so to their eventual expiation in blood and tears. Nor were there lacking distinguished writers to lend the authority of the latest philosophy to the primeval practice of self-indulgence. Mr. Bertrand Russell, a brilliant mathematician who had been imprisoned during the war as a pacifist, eloquently advocated increased sexual freedom. "I am sure," he declares in *Education and the Social Order*, "that university life would be better, both intellectually and morally, if most university students had temporary childless marriages." Many others who may not have been prepared to advocate casual sexual promiscuity propounded systems in which it was not difficult, for those who wished it, to find countenance for the instincts which prompted them to overthrow the barriers of social discipline. In a particularly popular series of broadcasts in the summer of 1930, Professor John

MacMurray expounded the creed that "there is no such thing as a moral law," "unless a man is able to make up his own mind what he himself wants . . . he is not free," and that "to be oneself freely and spontaneously, to realise oneself—that *is* to be a good man or woman." The professor was not of course commending the life of Spandrell to the young, but it is not difficult to see how a young man who was disposed to live the life of Spandrell might have supposed that he was receiving professorial authority for doing so. And indeed an impulse towards Spandrellism was certainly the general effect of that more academic and technical scientific and philosophical thinking which reached its public indirectly, by means of such intellectual middlemen as journalists, broadcasters and novelists. With the physicist explaining that no observation is valid save for a particular observer, the Marxist that no philosophy (including, presumably, the Marxist philosophy) is true except for a particular class at a particular time, and the Freudian that all morality and all beliefs (including, presumably, the Freudian) are but the product of suppressed sexual complexes, it was natural that the public to which these self-contradictory doctrines filtered down, should come insensibly to believe that there is no truth and no morality at all. If there is no absolute truth, and no absolute values, one way of life is as good, or as bad, as another, and neither is of any particular consequence. Henry the Eighth lived one kind of life, and St. Francis of Assisi another; that is all.

And certainly the life of Spandrell was lived upon a steadily increasing scale. Unlike crime, morals cannot be statistically measured, but there happen to be statistics about marriage, and marriage is so much the centre, and the touchstone, of the moral stability of a nation that these have a special significance. In 1918 there were more divorces than there had ever been before, and in 1919 there were half as many again. In 1928 more than four thousand decrees *nisi* were made absolute. Not only had marriage ceased to be a sacrament; the marriage vows, taken under circumstances of the utmost conceivable solemnity, were now widely treated with much the same off-hand cynicism as the dictators have since so often shown towards their own solemn undertakings. Divorce, however, partly no doubt for economic reasons, was never common among the poor. And this was symptomatic. Perversion, increasingly prevalent, if report be true, on the stage and in certain other small artistic and intellectual coteries, was virtually unknown among the working-classes. The post-war *dégringolade* in fact was the sudden decadence of a very small, if very conspicuous, subsection of society. The moral collapse was largely confined to the over-publicised idle rich and the intellectuals; and by intellectuals I do not mean, I need hardly say, men and women with intellects; I mean men and women mature in intelligence but immature in character or experience. It was of them that Hermann Rauschning wrote, "Those who regard themselves as the forces of progress are in truth forces of retrogression." This minority, however, though insignificant in numbers, was both vocal and extremely conspicuous, so that, as with the Court society of the Restoration, it was dangerously easy to mistake it for the nation. Moreover from its very nature it was influential out of all proportion to its numbers.

§9

Such was the wider offensive, a tacit assumption in everyday life that the line of least resistance was the wise man's course, that courage, loyalty, discipline and endurance were outmoded relics of an over-exacting past, and that no modern need be ashamed to profess their counterparts, bad faith, cowardice, self-indulgence or surrender. This, if the fashion of softness had lasted long enough among the vocal few, would have come nearest to infecting the unvocal many. And here and there there were sporadic and grotesque attempts deliberately to uproot the fundamental virtues; a curious twentieth-century reversal of the proverbially vain attempt to make men virtuous by Act of Parliament. Seen against the moral background of the 'twenties and 'thirties, such efforts had the advantage of protective colouring, and seemed almost rational to many contemporary observers. Thus it was an essential tenet of the pacifist creed at this time that any preparation for war, however modest, was wrong, not only because it was considered, oddly enough, to make war more likely ("Armaments mean war" proved a successful election cry), but because it roused martial passions in the impressionable young; and the League of Nations Union and the Fellowship of Reconciliation both did their best to abolish the annual Air Display at Hendon. They may have thought that it would infect school-children with a desire to butcher foreigners. Also, no doubt, they found it shocking, and, like the Victorian spinster who fitted green baize trousers to the naked legs of her dining-room table, they were anxious to cover up what shocked them. The Labour City Council at Sheffield refused to allow the King's Yorkshire

Dragoons to drill on the Langley Housing Estate, and abolished the Officers Training Corps at King Edward the Sixth's School. City fathers similarly minded pursued the same tactics, abolishing or discouraging O.T.C's, Empire Day celebrations and territorial drill or recruiting. It is not altogether surprising that Fuehrer and Duce, viewing this island from afar, and through the distorting lenses of their own secret ambitions, should have persuaded themselves that Britain would soon be an easy prey. A widely discussed resolution passed by the Union at Oxford, and other Universities, to the effect that members would decline to fight for King and country, did much to confirm our observant enemies in their dangerous illusion. They were naturally unaware that, so far from representing the youth of England, these debating clubs did not even represent their own Universities, or that many of those who voted for their ill-considered motion were in fact merely registering a pious hope that the next war, if there was to be one, would be waged by the League of Nations. The pacifists had not in fact succeeded in turning young England soft. Paradoxically, indeed, it is highly doubtful whether, as a body, they were even soft themselves. For the hundred and thirty thousand members claimed by the Peace Pledge Union in 1937 were a very different proposition from the handful of artists and intellectuals who had evaded the last war, and set the fashion of sneering at it afterwards. Morally and intellectually, the hundred and thirty thousand were a very heterogeneous collection. Some were sincere and courageous idealists, capable of intelligent controversy, and morally the salt of the earth. Others, a great deal more numerous, were probably, it is true, merely rationalising their own personal fears of war. But the majority were simply honest citizens in an advanced state of mental confusion, who had persuaded themselves that by taking pledges and passing resolutions they could somehow dissociate themselves from a future war, for all the world as if a man were to vote that he would have nothing to do with cancer. Indeed, largely owing to the equivocal association with it of the Communist party, there was actually a well-marked strain of belligerency in British pacifism. If these were sheep they were curiously aggressive sheep. Thus the deliberations of an Anti-War Congress held at Amsterdam in 1932, with numerous Communists among its members, were far from meek in character, and its slogans, "Stop the brigandage of Japan," "Break the Fascist Terror," suggested that, so far from being a negation of force, pacifism was a militant policy of aggression. Quite a number of youthful pacifists betook themselves to Spain during the civil war, to fight for whatever objects were then being pursued there by the Comintern. A certain proportion of these young gentlemen, it is true, have tended to revert, since their own country has been involved in war, to their earlier pacifist professions, but these vagaries, though they certainly point to a deficiency of logic, and even of patriotism, can hardly be said to suggest cowardice. Even the once conspicuously bellicose littérateurs of the Left who sought asylum in the United States after the outbreak of the European war for which they had clamoured, had some of them once followed the guns to Spain or China. In brief, although the moral disintegration which followed the last war involved a number of pacifists or shirkers, compensating themselves for an uneasy complex of inferiority by sneering at the ordinary men who had shamed them, and the virtues they did not possess, yet pacifism as an organised movement, though it attracted the flabby, was by no means flabby itself. And, like the post-war *dégringolade*, it was an affair of the cultured few, and not of the uncultured many. Among the few was undoubtedly a sediment of genuine decadence; a military interviewing officer reported, after a year of interviewing recruits for the Army, that of the conscientious objectors who reached him (having been rejected by the tribunals) scarcely ten per cent were of the wage-earning class, and something like ninety per cent were morally or physically inferior specimens. A rot, it may be concluded, had set in; but it had not had time to spread far before it was overtaken by a new tragedy. Not so far as to doom us when the test came. Not so far but that we could recover, under fire.

§ 10

In every country which, after being spiritually poisoned by materialism, lost the flower of its youth in the war, there was bound to be abnormality of some sort in the post-war decades. In Germany it became the vaster abnormality of thugs and bullies who, after they had seized power, were able to imprint their savagery upon an entire state. But there, too, there had been, under the republic of Weimar, a campaign against the moral and intellectual foundations of Christendom, darker and more desperate in degree, yet not so dissimilar in kind, from its British counterpart. Of the way in which the Weimar regime prepared the way for Hitler, Dr. Rauschning writes:

"A whole nation had lost its moral and intellectual foundation. It was delivering itself up to the most atrocious substitutes, to a world of substitutes that permitted it to cast aside all the moral institutions of civilised life. But what was responsible for this sort of thing? The few post-war years and the mass propaganda of this one party of Nazism? That is a grotesque shifting of responsibility. . . . For three generations, ninety years, and indeed, for one hundred and fifty or two hundred years, a so-called ' German ' has been trained up. For ninety years the materialist conception of history has worked hard to spread among the masses its shallow stupid materialism, and to praise this as progress. For three generations, the political Left Wing in Germany has been at work to destroy Christianity, and now do they want to disown their product? It *is* their product." [1]

Hitler has become the most terrible of enemies to the family, but his talk, in the Weimar period, of saving it won him some support, precisely because there were so many advanced persons in Germany speaking of family life as one more prison to be broken down. In Britain, and in other victorious countries, it was the lesser abnormality of a streak of softness and defeatism, "too many writers," as Mr. St. John Ervine put it, who have "cultivated despair and the spirit of defeat, until it has become a habit, a piece of routine, the easiest thing a sloppy undergraduate can do." And there were those other factors at work which tended to produce similar results in a dozen different countries. A "mental climate," for one thing, to which softness came naturally; for the characteristic *virtue* of our age was kindness, as that of other ages has been courage or faith or chastity, and the perversion, as Aristotle would say, of kindness is softness,

[1] Heimann Rauschning, *Make & Break with the Nazis,* 159.

just as the perversion of courage is brutality. Moreover there is the long process to be remembered by which, since the French Revolution, power has been transferred from the military classes to the merchants and writers and speakers—from those who were best at facing bullets to those who were best at influencing ballots—so that a war, with its temporary return of the soldier to power and prestige, appears something specially contrary to the course of nature and the laws of progress. And there is that divorce, common just now in all countries which share our pattern of civilisation, between intellect and experience, which produces what, for lack of a better label, we call the intellectual, and Napoleon called the ideologue, a type which may almost be said to date from the French Revolution. The slow poison of materialism for a century, and then the sudden slaughter of most of those who were best fitted to resist the effects of the poison, in the United States, too—which in the last war, out of its vaster population, lost less than an eighth of our total of killed, but has harboured the virus of material-ism in an even acuter form—forces such as these have bred an acuter onset of the same symptoms as our own. As a writer in the *New York Herald Tribune* put it, in August, 1941:

" Something fatal and subversive is undermining the morale of the nation. It began years ago when his-torians . . . sought to demonstrate that the United States was wrong in resisting Germany in the World War. It began when pacifists shrieked against the horrors of war and taught the younger generation to avoid honour and courage as well. . . . The American people . . . are fast losing the capacity for moral indignation. . . . They are willing to let others

fight for our freedom and the safety of democracy. . . .
Nothing can save America short of a great moral and
spiritual awakening."

And here is a passage of characteristically hearty denunciation of a phenomenon only too familiar to ourselves,
from a recent American work, Mr. Lawrence Hunt's
A Letter to the American People:

"You have probably noticed with mingled amusement
and disgust those intellectuals who are sophomoric in
their sensitivity to criticism from the outside world.
They loudly, bitterly and often properly denounce
statesmen, judges, big businessmen. But if some of
their own group are in turn similarly attacked they
yell bloody murder. . . . I think this sensitivity of
certain intellectuals is partly caused by another
sophomoric mental state—a belief that they are
mentally superior to those of us, for example, who
earn our living as businessmen or lawyers. They are
obviously more articulate, they know more words, and
quite probably they got 'better marks' in school or
college than those engaged on more vulgar pursuits.
And they cling, at times rather frantically, to their
adolescent belief in themselves and a comforting scorn
towards the rest of us. It's a strange priesthood they've
created and its creed seems to be criticism with im-
punity toward all, immunity from criticism by any. . . .
"I think . . . that our academic friends will probably
admit, in private, that the greatest weakness of their
great profession is that its members are rarely compelled
to make decisions which have definite and almost
immediate consequences. The businessman and lawyer
must make those decisions constantly in order to carry

54

on. Naturally many wrong decisions are made, but partly as a result of making them a reasonable degree of tolerance is shown towards those who make them and suspicion and contempt are felt for the intellectual perfectionist who does not make decisions, but bewails the wrong ones. . . .

"Whatever the reason, the so-called 'leaders of American thought' failed as leaders. . . . Archibald MacLeish with winning sincerity and melancholy charm admitted in effect that he and his fellow intellectuals had been damn' fools in playing the cynic rather than the man during the last twenty years."

Any one who has broken a lance with intellectuals in any country will probably agree with Mr. Hunt that, though their chief interest, and often indeed their profession, may be criticism of others, they are bitterly resentful of the slightest criticism of themselves, believing, it would seem, that in a modern democracy nothing should be immune from criticism, save the critics. Indeed if for once the humility, or indifference, with which the public customarily accepts their strictures is varied by the mildest counter-attack, their customary cold rationalism is apt to be quickly swept away by a surge of confused and angry emotion. I have argued for an hour on end with intellectuals about intellectuals, and at the end of it all, have found them, not, I think, entirely owing to my fault, still apparently under the impression that I was attacking intellect. Let me therefore close what has been, I am afraid, a tiresome chapter, dealing, as it has had to deal, with what will soon itself be a closed volume in our history, by repeating that the more intellect the better. No community can prosper if it lacks powerful intelligences. Only, if the community is indeed to prosper, they must be wedded to character and experience. Intelligence divorced from character and experience, intelligence in a partial vacuum, becomes a prey to numerous maladies, some few of which I have attempted to describe. In the course of the next two chapters I shall have something to say of some of the means of ensuring that intellect does not suffer this tragic divorce. But already, in the harsh climate of war-time, the intellectual, as we knew him in the 'twenties and 'thirties, is vanishing from the scene. New spiritual forces are abroad. His successor, it is safe to prophesy, will be less despairing, less timid—and less materialist. Here is a valedictory to the intellectuals from Mr. Julian Duguid's remarkable *I am Persuaded*:

"The road is no longer blocked, as it was for me at one period, by the tyranny of the intellectual. . . . The mental inhabitants of Bloomsbury have had their day of sneering. Ignorant of all but books, unskilled to work with their hands, they kissed and told and faded. In the harsh glare of war, they made room for better men. Still, they served a purpose in their time. By their acid attacks on religion, by their open contempt for the spirit, they compelled the seeker after truth to look to his own foundations." [1]

[1] Julian Duguid, *I am Persuaded*, 150.

III

NOT EXAMINEES, BUT MEN

§ 1

MORALE, which is to say morals, is the foundation of successful war, as of successful civilisation. The first stages of a second world war have surely shewn that, despite all, the British still possess formidable reserves of courage, loyalty, discipline and endurance. Despite certain obvious exceptions, the indisputable fact remains that, in the mass, the British have displayed that tough fundamental resilience which is compounded of courage, loyalty, endurance and discipline. These basic virtues alone, needless to say, will not win a war, but it is certain that no war can be won without them. In this critical moment, poised between a past darkened by wasted opportunities and an obscure future, whose whole nature depends upon our turning present suffering to good account, we shall not deserve to survive unless we resolve that these fundamental virtues shall be preserved, prized and developed, both now and in the years to come. For unless it is certain that after the war we shall be fit, as victors, to imprint them on that new civilisation which it will be the victors' inescapable destiny to shape, what right have we to look for victory? In this respect, as in others, it is our business both to foresee and to will. We have both to perceive clearly those forces already taking shape around us, which are the future in embryo, and to determine how, with the help of Providence, we shall best release, strengthen and enrich them in the years ahead.

§ 2

This is one of several spheres in which the national
methods of education are of basic importance. One far-
reaching evolutionary modification of them, though not
actually yet effected, is already clearly visible on the
horizon. The public schools, as we call them, have
hitherto been the most significant element in our
educational system, partly because they have been the
training-ground of our rulers, partly because, in the
sphere of education, they are the one distinctively English
invention, often copied but nowhere reproduced. With
taxation rising to nineteen shillings and sixpence in the
pound, and the owners of fixed incomes, as always,
hardest hit, it is clear that the class which could once
afford to pay for the expensive privilege of sending its
children to the public schools will soon cease to be able
to do so. For the schools state assistance will be the only
alternative to gradual extinction. And state assistance
will only be accorded on conditions. These, it is to
be hoped, will not include state control. The individuality
and variety of the schools, and the high standard of their
teaching staffs, would be unlikely to survive bureaucratic
centralisation. One condition of state assistance, however, is bound to be free places for children from the state
elementary schools. And once the principle of free places
has been accepted, the proportion of free places is likely
steadily to increase. Within the near future there will be
a new kind of school in the inner citadel of the British
social and educational system. What kind of school is it
to be?

This much is obvious. It will no longer be the exclusive
preserve of a prosperous minority. The classrooms will

no longer be *class* rooms. The principal vice of the
public school, its privileged exclusiveness, will progres-
sively disappear. But this, when all is said and done, will
be a mainly negative change, and does not take us so
far as some enthusiasts suppose. The public schools
might well shed their exclusiveness, and yet, so far from
improving in quality, might then atrophy into inferior
and colourless relics of what Spengler would have called
their "active" phase. Fortunately the analogy of the
powerful, and little understood, influence which they
exercised in the latter half of the nineteenth century
suggests some very different conclusions as to the part
which they may yet play in the latter half of the twentieth.
The predominant virtue, and the chief characteristic, of
the public-school tradition has always been the emphasis
it has placed on the training of character. Even at a time
when little was taught but the Greek and Latin classics,
when there was no physical training, no handwork, nor
even any organised games (but, some will say, when all
these needs were almost as adequately met by the boys
themselves in their very considerable spare time), even
then the public schools never made the mistake of
supposing that education consists solely of book-learning
and the passing of examinations—as did the over-logical
French who, when the supreme test came, found that not
enough Frenchmen were prepared to accept responsibility.
Arnold of Rugby, who for present purposes may be said
to have made the public schools in the eighteen thirties,
set himself to turn out "Christian gentlemen," two labels
less in fashion now than then. What he meant by
"Christian" we need not now consider, but his "gentleman" was a term with an historical significance which
concerns us very closely. During the nineteenth century
the new middle-class was coming into its own. The

industrial revolution had given it economic power, the Reform Act political power; the public schools were now to add social status. Socially the eighteenth century was still feudal; in relation to the noble landowner, the doctor, the lawyer, the banker and the parson occupied much the same equivocal status as the veterinary surgeon or the village schoolmaster to-day; they would hardly expect to be invited to stay to dinner. By the end of the nineteenth century the social gulf had been bridged: all of them were going to the same public schools. Duke and doctor both belonged to the same new class; they were both gentlemen. The public schools, in short, had been the principal instrument of the social ascent of the middle classes. It is interesting to note that the philosophy of that period of insurgence had been Liberal Individualism, and to this day there are two well-marked types of public school, those, with Eton as their prototype, modelled, with a faint swagger, on the aristocratic tradition which descends from before the Reform Act and the rise of the middle classes, and those, for which Rugby has served as model, which represent the sound and sober ideals of the Victorian middle classes. Up to a comparatively recent date it was still possible to distinguish to which of the two types a school belonged by the simple test of whether it played Rugby football or not.

But if socially the public schools, and the ideal of the gentleman which they fostered, were the power which fused the new commercial and professional upper middle class and the old landowning aristocracy into one much more heterogeneous, yet moderately coherent, social stratum, educationally and morally they were responsible for an almost equally striking transformation. For it was during the nineteenth century, and as an integral part of the social ascent of the middle classes, and the diffusion of the ideal of the gentleman, that the present high standards of professional integrity were evolved. In the eighteenth century the lawyer and the doctor, not to mention the banker, were often pretty disreputable rascals. In the nineteenth century the professions developed new and exacting codes of conduct, mainly directed to ensuring that their members rendered conscientious and dis-interested service to the public. Professional men, in short, were expected to behave like gentlemen. The new code even partially succeeded in penetrating the world of commerce; the standards of the educated Victorian business-man were usually rigid, if narrow. But the world of commerce was too vast, its denizens too numerous and heterogeneous, too constantly recruited from below or from abroad, for the new professional ideals to root themselves extensively there. And to-day, whatever the new style of idealistic advertisement—"our motto is service"—may claim, the motive force of industry and commerce as a whole is certainly not exclusively what the motive force of the professions may be said to have become, disinterested service to the community. This is true not only of employers and shareholders, but of the trade unions, which were equally susceptible to the prevailing materialism of the nine-teenth century, and, despite the simplicity and integrity of most of their members, have frequently, as organis-ations, regarded their own interests as more important than those of the community, or indeed of other trade unions.

It may be added here that, in addition to the part they played in establishing new codes of professional morality, the public schools had no difficulty in transferring to the new class of gentlemen the old soldierly ideals of courage and service which the feudal aristocracy had developed during the centuries in which they led their men into battle. The following tribute was addressed particularly to the older British aristocracy, and the part it played in the last war, but everything said here is equally applicable to the newer "gentlemen," whose names appear with those of the most ancient families on the war memorials of the same public schools, and is all the more remarkable in that it comes from the pen of the Radical Charles Masterman, Mr. Lloyd George's chief lieutenant in the land campaign directed against the very men whom he is here applauding:

"There are books, some written privately, some published, which describe how these men met the terrific challenge of almost certain death. Among those who had entered the Army itself and had dawdled away their time pig-sticking in India or polo-playing in South Africa, the thing came with a great sense of relief. If they did not woo darkness as a bride, they at least realised that all their life had been moulded for this hour, and many went into battle singing, without a trace of fear. They fought; if they were wounded, they returned as speedily as possible to the front; they allowed no health certificates to interfere with their ardour. Some knew with certainty that they would be killed, but cared nothing so long as they were facing the enemy. In the retreat from Mons and the first battle of Ypres perished the flower of the British aristocracy; 'playing the game' to the last as they had been taught to play it all through their days of boyhood. They earned the devotion of their men, and, you may say with confidence, nine-tenths of them thought of their men first. . . . In the useless slaughter of the Guards on the Somme, or of the Rifle Brigade in Hooge Wood, half the great families of England, heirs of large estates and wealth, perished without a cry. These boys, who had been brought up with a prospect before them of every good material thing that life can give, died without complaint, often through the bungling of Generals, in a foreign land. And the British aristocracy perished, as they perished in the Wars of the Roses, or in fighting for their King in the great Civil War, or as the Southern aristocracy in America, in courage and high effort and an epic of heroic sacrifice, which will be remembered so long as England endures."

It is the *ethos* which is capable at times of crisis of flowering into devotion of this high order, which has been particularly assailed by the malcontent intellectual.

Here we come to the real significance of the analogy which suggests itself with the part played by the public schools in the last century. In the last century the public schools served, incidentally, as an instrument of the social advance of the middle class; in this century the new public schools will serve, incidentally, as an instrument of the social advance of the wage-earning class. In the last century they were largely responsible for the creation of a new class, compounded of the old feudal aristocracy and the new commercial and professional middle class, and more or less represented by the "gentleman," a word which had now become a social label as well as a moral judgment. In this century there is no reason why they should not play a central part in the extension of that class, destined now to be increasingly recruited from the lowest economic strata of society, into a new social aggregate whose gradual fusion (if it does not prove too comprehensive to wear a label at all) may well again proceed beneath the now time-honoured label of "gentleman." In the last century the appearance of the gentleman as a new social phenomenon meant also a new moral phenomenon, the extension of "gentlemanly" conduct through the new professional codes. In the new century the new schools will doubtless help to extend the notion of gentlemanly conduct, of the professional ideal of service, further than these have yet penetrated, into the realm of industry and commerce—a process which can only be assisted by the inevitable transformation of further competitive undertakings into some form of public service. All this forecast of the significance of the new schools in the new age depends, it will be seen, upon the public schools themselves carrying over into the new phase their traditional emphasis upon the training of character—or perhaps it would be more accurate to say, their training in citizenship. The value of this asset, which may be sacrificed if we do not deliberately decide to preserve it, is almost incalculable.

" . . . the greatest instrument of social education in England . . . is the so-called public school, which should rather be called the residential school. Whatever its weaknesses, it has by its very nature one great value. It is an incomparable school of social education, of citizenship, where boys learn citizenship by being citizens. That is what a public school boy is—a citizen. He has two countries—his school, a community of perhaps 600 boys, and his house, a community of some 50 boys. He is a member, a citizen of both these communities, and in each of them has his place and privileges and duties. He lives inside them for eight months in the year. Their problems, their interests,

their happenings are before his mind on every day
of these eight months. Never in later life will he be so
intensely a member of a community, never again will
he live so completely in and for a community, as he
does in those school years. Living thus as a citizen he
imbibes instinctively the fundamental principles of
good citizenship. To feel yourself part of a community
which you have a share and a responsibility in making,
whose successes are somehow your successes and whose
failures cast their shadow on you—to be able to obey
and to live and to co-operate with other members of
the community—this is the essence of citizenship, and
this the boy at a good residential school learns unconsciously every day of his life, not by being taught
it, but by practising it. Schools or trade unions may
be narrowed to serve the interests or represent the views
of a class. But this is not inherent in their nature, nor
do these incidental weaknesses alter the fact that they
create a spirit which may serve wider uses." [1]

It is indeed this peculiar merit in the public, or residential,
schools which has made of them the one English invention
in education which has provoked interest and imitation
all over the world. Whatever the educational pattern of
the new age may be, it will be sheer destructive loss if
this special virtue is no longer to be found at the heart
of it, far more widely available, but in essence unaltered.
Like the trade unions, the public schools have devoted
themselves too narrowly to the interests of a class, but,
like the trade unions, they have been a great training-
ground of citizenship. In every civilised country in the
world critics would be found to endorse the verdict of a
distinguished American:

[1] *The Future of Education* (Anon.), *The Round Table*, September, 1941.

" Few countries can boast as high a type of manhood as that produced by the public schools of England. The courage, tact, coolness of judgment, political insight, intellectual attainments and administrative ability of an Englishman of this class is not less amazing for his studied moderation and his practised efforts to belittle personal accomplishments. I have seen Englishmen go out to rule provinces from which their predecessors had not returned—and do so with no more outward concern than if they were taking a joy-ride. I recall a newly wed Scotch couple that went out to the Sudan-Abyssinia frontier a day or two after the news arrived that the party of engineers the husband was supposed to join had been murdered. I have seen Englishmen walk into the jaws of death among bitterly hostile crowds, and with patience, tact, coolness gradually gain control." [1]

Yes, like the trade unions, although they may have devoted themselves too narrowly to the interests of a class, the public schools have been a great training-ground of citizenship, and it will be the business of a new age, not to destroy the training-ground, but to turn the citizenship to wider ends. Nevertheless it is certain that powerful influences will seek to jettison this, with every other relic of the public school tradition. It is a curious reflection that about one British citizen in five hundred would probably be unable to read that tribute of Mr. Viton's to the product of the public schools without indignation and resentment. And this sort of critic, though far from typical, is exceptionally vocal. Indeed criticism of the public schools has never been more insistent and contemptuous than during the last decade,

[1] Albert Viton, *Great Britain*, 330.

when the schools were at the height of their popularity, and to many of them a boy could hardly expect admission unless his name was entered at birth; and it has been largely directed against the training of character either by those who disliked, or envied, the character which the training was intended to produce, or by those who professed to believe that education should decline to concern itself actively with character at all. Such criticisms have been to some extent reinforced by the example of new, experimental schools, which have deliberately reduced to vanishing-point any interference with the uncontrolled development of the natural instincts of the child. Pupils at these select, and sometimes expensive, seminaries might wear verminous underclothing or plot, and execute, ingenious burglaries in their spare time; what matter? Let nature take her course. The fact that in nature even the higher animals have to discipline their offspring to train them for their environment—birds are "cruel" to their young, to teach them to fly—was overlooked by the apostles of "nature." But perhaps, given the mental climate of its period, the only really surprising feature of this pedagogue's version of the ancient but resurgent cult of do as you please was the characteristic assumption that it was a newly discovered form of progress, since, to adapt an observation of G. K. Chesterton's, it is difficult to see that this particular line of least resistance any more represents a new principle in education than sleeping under a hedge represents a new form of architecture. Yes, there may well be determined resistance to any attempt to maintain and modernise in the new schools the tradition of deliberate character-training which should be their legacy from the old. Yet there are further reasons, not legacies of the past but inherent in the future, reasons of the utmost importance,

why the schools of the future should insist upon extending
education much further beyond mere book-learning than
it has ever reached in the past.

§ 3

The new schools, it is already obvious, will be expected
to provide what is usually described as a ladder of opportunity. A not inconsiderable ladder there already is.
More than a third of the undergraduates in the two ancient
and once exclusive Universities already come from the
state-conducted elementary schools by means of state,
county, municipal and other scholarships. It is already
easier for the brilliant son of a miner to reach Oxford
than for the brilliant son of a clergyman. But the nation
has not at this moment so many outstanding leaders that
it need be tempted to rest content with the methods of
selection, whether by education, big business or trade
unions, now in vogue. Who would maintain that every
member of the present War Cabinet is a man of outstanding mental and moral distinction? We may assume,
I think, that the war will have reminded a good many of
those who needed reminding, that democracy needs
leadership, and the corollary of leadership, discipline.
The notion that, tainted by association with the *Fuehrer
prinzip*, these fundamental qualities have somehow become undemocratic was one of the more dangerous and
degenerate heresies of the last twenty years. The nation
will want leaders, and it will certainly expect to be freer
than it is at present to look for them in every nook and
cranny of society. Up to a point the denser the traffic up,
and down, the ladder the better, certainly, for society.
Up to a point—for I note in passing that the importance

of promiscuous ladder-climbing tends to be exaggerated by writers who have unreflectingly inherited the righteous rage of nineteenth-century Radicals against jobbery, "placemen" and privilege. Now that so many of the barriers of privilege are already down, it is probably true that a very considerable majority of the nation is not interested in ladder-climbing at all. And this is all to the good. A fiercely competitive childhood under the shadow of the ladder is very far from the Christian tradition, a joyless and elbowing existence at the best, and a society without boundaries, a society in constant flux, is no society at all. A healthy and growing community must have roots; and the completely organised restlessness of the Victorian Radical's dream would probably be national suicide. The experiment indeed has nowhere yet been attempted, and probably never will be: in the revolutionary states of the twentieth century, whether Communist or Fascist, the ladder is very strictly reserved for a numerically insignificant, but highly privileged, minority, the members of the Party. And it is clear that British history owes very much to the men who have pursued hereditary callings, generation after generation manning the lifeboats or the mines, serving in Navy or Army or Church. It is as though one lifetime was not sufficient to furnish complete mastery of such exacting pursuits, and, following his forebears into them, a man could count upon drawing on the accumulated aptitudes of past generations. Ancestral memory, after all, is a familiar enough phenomenon. It is everywhere evident in the animal world—in the migrating swallows crossing the Mediterranean by the devious route which ages ago, before the Mediterranean sea existed, was a line of land, or the birds which build their nests without ever having seen one built. Nor is it less apparent in man. It takes four or five generations, it is said, to make a diamond-cutter. The son of a Lancashire cotton-spinner, who had never seen Lancashire or a cotton-mill till he was twenty, has been known to handle his first piece of cloth with the peculiar technique of his craft. Samuel Butler (who, since he enjoys considerable literary prestige, is usually treated as a spiritual forerunner by the Marxists of to-day, but was in fact a convinced Conservative) founded his Conservatism largely on the belief, expounded in his *Life and Habit*, that the instinctive knowledge which man inherits from the past is more valuable than the conscious knowledge which he deliberately acquires during his own lifetime. If heredity is more potent than environment, a people which learned to look down on a man who followed his father's calling would be deliberately cutting away the roots of its own most valuable qualities. There are qualities peculiar, too, to the man born to his station, high or low, even as to the man who makes his own way. The King is not necessarily inferior to the President, or the Marquis of Salisbury to the American millionaire. Nevertheless we may take it for certain that as long as our people remain free we shall expect to maintain an increasing volume of traffic on the ladder. Here as elsewhere it will be a question of compromise—between the rootless fluidity of a society universally and perpetually on the make and the unimaginative traditionalism of a nation of heirs apparent.

§ 4

If, therefore, as will be expected of them, the schools of the future are to choose us our leaders more effectively than ever before, let it be recorded at once that the system of examination in book learning now practised will have to be abandoned for ever. At present, in the state schools, an examination in book knowledge at the age of eleven determines a boy's educational fate for ever. Even if it were deferred, as has been suggested, to thirteen, or, for that matter, to any other age, a test of this kind would be all but useless for a community in search of leadership. In a book examination at thirteen, or twenty-one, it is probable that Shakespeare and Cromwell and Nelson and, in all probability, Mr. Winston Churchill himself, would have been ignominiously ploughed. The successful examinee, whom the present restricted system of education trains for advancement through the present restricted system of examination, is usually the candidate who can most readily absorb, and most lucidly reproduce, other people's ideas. He need not possess courage, common sense, an original mind, or a sound physique. Of all the qualifications for leadership only one, a very important one, no doubt, but nevertheless only one, is required of him. In an examination for future librarians and literary critics this might not matter, but in an examination for future Prime Ministers and administrators it matters very much indeed. Most of us have met the colourless absorbent of ideas, the inevitable laureate of the examination-room, whom no one, who knew him, would trust to manage a whelk-stall for a week, but whom the last of many triumphs too often lands in the Civil Service for life. More often than not in youth a strong character or an original mind will act as non-conductors for other people's ideas, and after a few years at the bottom of his class the potential Rhodes or Washington may leave school, officially classified as backward, perhaps for life-long obscurity.

There is already a ladder of educational opportunity which within the last twenty-five years has completely transformed the character of the ancient Universities, and whose rungs are State, and Local Education Authority, Scholarships. What it now needs are not merely, as is usually assumed, more rungs, but different ones. Too often, as the present Master of Balliol has put it, successful competitors reach the University "undeveloped in body and in mind. . . . For, under the present system at any rate, to be trained from early youth to think about nothing but examinations is an experience which only the strongest mind can survive." To put it more bluntly, we have been spending too much trouble and money on producing too many callow, unenterprising and self-centred young examination-*wallahs* as the raw material of our future leaders. We have in fact been purchasing the democratisation of the Universities with the creation of an intelligentsia, in the worst sense of that ambiguous term.

Here, the public school is not, of course, the chief delinquent. No boy could pass as a boarder through a public school without acquiring a wider education than books alone could provide him with. Indeed, as we have seen, the chief hope of the new schools is that they should inherit the traditional interest of their predecessors in the growth of character. But public school tradition is not enough. In fact, though they have done more than any other national institution to produce leadership, the public schools have themselves unintentionally done a great deal to swell the ranks of that sterile intelligentsia which during the last twenty years has proved a principal breeding-ground of moral defeatism. Most of them have permitted, or encouraged, the tradition that in that system of self-government which they inherited from Arnold, and have more or less unconsciously developed into a great school of character, responsibility is best exercised by athletes. Too often this perversion of the Arnold tradition—for Arnold made the sixth form his oligarchy—has proved a heresy, and a line of least resistance, which has done more than has been generally recognised to nullify the services of the schools themselves to the community. For though leadership does not depend upon brains alone, it does not depend upon character alone, either; and though the hefty forward and the hawk-eyed batsman, whom the young are so ready to admire and obey, may obviously enough lack brains, it does not by any means necessarily follow that they possess character. Meanwhile, excluded from early responsibility and prestige, the unmuscular but intelligent adolescent, half envious, half contemptuous of the somewhat bovine school oligarchy, too often grows up with an exaggerated bias towards criticism and opposition, a constitutional suspicion of authority, and an irresistible tendency to overvalue the quick wits he possesses, and to underestimate the practical experience which he has not been allowed to acquire. Mr. Arnold Lunn has frankly recorded[1] how athletocracy, "the dictatorship of the Barbarians," at Harrow indoctrinated him with the instinct of revolt:

"Bolshevism is a revolutionary movement, the unavowed object of which is to replace the dictatorship

[1] *Come What May*, 37.

of the Barbarians by the dictatorship of the intellectuals, and my own boyish reverence for the Barbarians
was qualified by a Bolshie streak of incipient revolt
against the standards of a society which relegated me
to the lowest standards of the social hierarchy."

If he is specially unlucky, and fortune does not soon
supply him with a corrective, the intelligent adolescent
who has been excluded from the school aristocracy may
even develop into an incurable No man, nursing far
into maturity a secret inferiority complex, for which
Generals and Cabinet Ministers and Personages in general
are but the prefects of his school days somewhat over
life size, and evoke all the old mingling of envy and
contempt. Once made free of the intoxicating im-
munities of print, he will compensate himself for many
secret humiliations by the boldness of his assaults on
anything which he associates with them. This tendency
in the schools to produce a small minority of uneasy and
disappointed intellectuals would have mattered less,
were it not for the social and economic forces which not
only overstock the market with clever young men,
but prodigiously overreward success in industry and
commerce, while often leaving solid achievement in the
arts and the professions more or less unrecognised.
Combined with the mental distortions produced by a
public scholarship system restricted to book-learning,
the result of first training a small minority of highly
intelligent schoolboys into potential malcontents, and
then condemning a good many of them to further
frustration in later life, has been to create in this country
the small but unmistakable nucleus of something like a
British analogy to the Babu class, voluble, unpractical,
hypersensitive and resentful. If we tend to think well of

74

institutions which think well of us, we are equally inclined to think ill of those in which our undoubted abilities are not recognised.

"Vanity is the most potent of forces in the shaping of life and in the choice of political creeds. We tend to think well of institutions which think well of us. The man who is born into a family with a long tradition of distinguished service to the State derives some reflected glory from England's greatness, and tends to be a conservative. . . . If, on the other hand, your grandfather entered England in the 'fifties as an immigrant from south-eastern Europe, if you yourself are an intellectual with more brain than brawn, if you were kicked about at school by embryo Blimps, if you have no stomach for fighting and, in consequence, a detestation of war, you will naturally resent a criterion of values which assigns to you a low place at life's table." [1]

It is largely from among this small section of the community, itself recruited largely from the public schools, that the sustained campaign against the public school tradition, and the moral qualities associated with it, has been directed. Its ingrained bias against the Government has made of it something like a permanent opposition.

"Like the old Bolsheviks who were such a nuisance to the Communist Government of Russia, they have hardened into permanent and irresponsible opposition. They feel that it is not their business to ascertain the facts or to consider a question in all its bearings; and they believe that any attack on established order, however ignorant or ill-considered, is a battle fought

[1] Arnold Lunn, *Come What May*, 45.

for freedom; the mere act of faith involved in believing themselves to be on the side of progress exempts them from the duty of being practical." [1]

The new schools will certainly need to inherit their predecessors' special interest in character, but not, it is to be hoped, the bias against intelligence which still survives in their methods of self-government.

Here, as so often, it is not necessary to conjure a remedy out of the realms of imagination. A potential remedy is already inconspicuously at work, and needs only to be recognised, developed and extended. The County Badge Scheme, already in operation in various parts of the country, suggests a pattern for the education of the future. Here a boy is required to reach certain standards of physical performance—in running, jumping, throwing, swimming—to carry out an exploration, sail a boat, make something with his own hands. When all candidates climbing the early rungs of the scholarship ladder are required to show some such minimum of achievement beyond mere book-digestion, the foundations of the education of the future will have been laid. For the education of the future, the education which can find us leadership for this age of Blitzkriegs, must be the complete education of complete men and women. It is the illusion that human beings are mainly, if not merely, intelligences which has helped to saddle us with the predominance of the intellectual, the half-man whose intelligence is not founded upon character. Who has not encountered by now the zealous ideologue who cannot keep his own shoelaces tied up or find his razor in the morning, who can neither live happily with his wife nor pay his tailor, whose private life in fact has been laid

[1] Michael Roberts, *The Recovery of the West*, 210.

waste by timidity, selfishness or incompetence, but who is confidently prepared to organise British industry or plan world federation? Achievement does not depend upon mind alone, but upon mind, character and body, and complete education is education in all the qualities which are necessary for achievement. We are not fighting to make the world safe for the timid intellectual. The ladder of the future should be climbed by boys who show signs of initiative and *guts*, as well as of exceptional capacity for mental digestion. This is not to underrate the importance of intelligence. Intelligence is of sovereign importance, but unless intelligence is geared to character and experience, the mental engine races, futile and ultimately self-destructive. There are valuable lessons to be learnt from the Rhodes Scholarship system. The founder's object was to select young men who would be leaders, and he knew that all distinguished achievement depends upon a proper combination of intellect and character. He provided, therefore, in effect, that his scholars should be young men either of exceptional intelligence founded upon sound character, or of exceptional character founded upon sound intelligence. Neither quality alone would suffice. Of the two it is natural that selectors should be inclined to treat intelligence as the more important, if only because, in the existing examination system, there already exists a ready-made semi-scientific test of intelligence, whereas, although it is dangerously easy to mistake popularity or athletic prowess for conclusive evidence, no analogous laboratory test of character in fact exists. Some people might be disposed to add that the man of distinguished intelligence, who lacks character, is likely to achieve more than the man of distinguished character who lacks intelligence; he may become a scientist or a critic, while the dull-witted, however full of virtue and initiative, may remain a bank clerk all his life. But this is to overlook once more the indispensable share of character in all achievement. It is to exaggerate the importance of pure reason and to ignore that hinterland of the irrational which is evident in all greatness. A man does not become a Darwin or an Einstein without possessing powerful character: he does not choose a wife, a friend or even a new suit by reason alone. Moreover experience suggests that the man of strong character but small capacity for book-learning is in fact more, and not less, likely than the timid intellectual to make a success of life. In spite of which to choose either is a mistake. Naturally from time to time mistakes of this kind have been made by one or other of the numerous Rhodes Committees of Selection, scattered all over the British Commonwealth and the United States of America, but the election of an occasional cave man or ideologue has only served to emphasise the success of the system as a whole. There are statistics to show that a higher proportion of Rhodes Scholars than of open scholars from British schools, selected purely on an intelligence test, have obtained Firsts at Oxford, and, though here statistics are not available, it is highly probable that a higher proportion has also fulfilled the object of the Founder by afterwards achieving distinction in public service. The Rhodes system of selection suggests a pattern for the traffic on the educational ladder of the future, and therefore for the schools themselves. Education must be an even completer training of mind, body and character than it has been in the best of the public schools hitherto; it must be open to the whole community; and it must not make the dangerous old mistake of excluding many of the specially intelligent from early training in the use of authority.

Not Examinees, but Men

There has been another minor, but by no means unimportant, cause of that remoteness from reality which has made a section of the intelligentsia so easy a prey to exotic creeds and moral defeatism. Education keeps the prize boy too long out of the world. By the time he leaves the University at about twenty-two he may have been fourteen years or more in the cloisters. This may be to wear blinkers for too long. A young man too long accustomed to the study of abstract ideas and of impersonal forces, as artificially isolated by the lecture-room, may never afterwards manage to see things and people steadily and whole. Moreover this divorce between learning and experience has a profound effect upon education itself. Sir Richard Livingstone, in a wise chapter of *The Future of Education*, discusses some of the disadvantages of our habit of setting the young to study theory, without any practical experience of the facts to which theory relates. Aristotle himself pointed out that "a boy cannot be a philosopher" and that

"The young are not fit to be students of politics, for they have no experience of life and conduct, and it is these that supply the premises and subject matter of this branch of thought." [1]

The young can distinguish themselves in mathematics or music or linguistics, because these are abstract subjects. But philosophy, history and politics cannot be *understood* without experience of life. From the study of these subjects the young may acquire valuable mental discipline, they will learn relevance, proportion, style, they can, as Sir Richard Livingstone puts it, "play intellectual ping-pong with their tutors," but they cannot *understand* them. Education, he truly says, sorely needs what our present

[1] Aristotle Nicomachean Ethics i, 3, 5.

system almost wholly ignores, the cross-fertilisation of theory and experience. Theory illumines experience, and experience illumines theory. Newman maintains that, without experience, the young cannot *understand* literature.

> "Passages, which to a boy are but rhetorical common-places . . . at length come home to him, when long years have passed, and he has had experience of life, and pierce him, as if he had never before known them, with their sad earnestness and vivid exactness." [1]

There is a profound truth here. The significance of great literature gradually unfolds as one acquires the experience to penetrate it. As a boy I particularly admired those lines in the Odyssey which describe the living Odysseus' encounter, on his visit to the realm of the departed, with the shade of the great Achilles. Achilles asks for tidings of his son; Odysseus reassures him and "the spirit of Achilles, swift of foot, stalked with long strides along the lawns of asphodel, rejoicing in that I had told him of his son's high renown." As a boy I only knew that the Greek lines were strangely moving. I liked the long strides and the lawns of asphodel. Later, the poignancy of the great warrior's helpless exile among "the strengthless dead" impressed itself upon me, and his striding off into the shadows without a word of farewell. Later still, what moved me most was the picture of the father, suddenly happy in that grey place because of his son. In the same way, education will scatter seeds which must lie dormant until experience brings them to life. Until then, they remain *inert* ideas, and minds which even in maturity are deficient in experience will carry through life a dangerous burden of inert ideas.

[1] *Grammar of Assent*, 78. Both passages quoted by Sir Richard Livingstone.

For all these reasons there ought to be more cross-fertilisation of theory with experience during the long scholastic careers of those who are destined to be leaders of their generation. In particular, there ought to be (as the Master of Balliol has suggested) a year's break between school and university. If military conscription is still in force after the war, a year's discipline and physical training, rubbing shoulders with all sorts and classes, in the Army should make an invaluable prologue to the able schoolboy's University career, bringing the experience which will wake the inert idea to life, helping to turn the lecture-room into a mirror of reality, instead of a screen from it. That, unless the world is a much safer place than it is likely to become in our lifetime, we shall still have military conscription after the war is devoutly to be hoped. Quite apart from its military and diplomatic advantages, it represents a moral principle of deep significance. The claim of the state to exact this fundamental service from every citizen who enjoys its protection and privileges is profoundly in accord with the Socialist philosophy, and it is strange to recall that until well past the eleventh hour it was steadily denied by British Socialists. Conscription, however, need not be military. A year in the factories or on the land might do as much to toughen the physique, socialise the instincts and enrich the later learning of the young scholar as a year in one of the fighting services.

That the leaving-age in state elementary schools should be raised at least to fifteen, and that for three years after that there should be what has been called "educative control" of the adolescent, but that the best hope of educating the masses lies in residential adult schools on the Danish model, all this is a corollary of the extended search for leadership. But this chapter is not a treatise on education. I have merely been concerned to insist that, if we are to earn survival, not only by our continued possession of the fundamental virtues but by our capacity to imprint them on a new age, there are some traditions which must be maintained or modernised, and some which must be abandoned, at certain key points in our system.

IV

ENDS, AS WELL AS MEANS

§ 1

BUT we have not done with education. We have been thinking of the tough, fundamental virtues, courage, loyalty, discipline, endurance, without which a civilisation cannot defend itself. But there are virtues without which a civilisation is not worth defending. And can we, it may be asked, indeed claim to survive in order to perpetuate, and to imprint upon the age to come, the civilisation which we can see mirrored in the cheap Press, in cheap films and sex fiction, in jerry-built villas and quack medicines? Are we not bound to confess that the Progress of which we have boasted so glibly on platforms, the one deity in whom we have all so confidently believed, has meant little more in the last analysis than more wireless sets and better plumbing?

A blue-print of a New Social Order lately circulated by a popular weekly contained varied recipes for shorter hours and more wealth, for better hospitals and better houses, a Good Time, in short, for all. What it did not anywhere contain was any clear recognition of spiritual values. And yet if anything is obvious to-day, it is surely obvious that the world finds itself in its present plight precisely because for too long too many people have thought too exclusively in terms of a Good Time for themselves. We have created a civilisation rich in means, but almost destitute of Ends. We have been seeking some form of outer order, without having achieved inner order. A civilisation of means, but not of Ends: here surely is a creeping paralysis which must be cured, or of which some cure, implicit in resolve or conduct, must at least be in sight, if we are to earn survival. "Why are you fighting? To survive? Very well; but why should you survive?" Courage, loyalty, discipline, endurance—with these a civilisation may be strong enough to defend itself, but if it is to be worthy to survive it needs culture and it needs religion. And, in the supreme test, if it is not worthy to survive it will surely perish.

§ 2

A civilisation of means but not of Ends. An education which will maintain the virile fundamental qualities is not enough. We need an education which will concern itself with Ends, an education whose fruits will be something more than more wireless sets and better plumbing, an education which will not only teach us how to be mechanics or carpenters or accountants, but will set out to give us some notion of what Greek philosophers called "the good life." It is sometimes said that what we need is a liberal education for all. But we need, it will be found, more than that. A liberal education —though it is not entirely satisfactory, it is at any rate a familiar label, and it has the merit that we owe it, like so much else, to the Greek tradition in our civilisation. A liberal education was the education fit for a free man; and a free man, unlike a slave, was qualified to lead the good life. We are familiar enough with the contrast between a vocational and a liberal education. A vocational training, we should say, fits a man to earn his living in one particular calling, to be a mechanic or a carpenter or an accountant. A liberal education, on the other hand,

84

should fit him to lead a fuller and richer life, whatever his calling. Man is body, mind and character, and the training of any one of these three to help him to a richer, a more fully human, life is liberal education. To learn to box in order to acquire a quicker eye and a cooler temper is part of a liberal education—to learn to box in order to be able to knock down a rival is not. To learn French in order to be able to enjoy a holiday in France, is not a liberal education; to learn French in order to study a historic civilisation, is. But the distinction between means and ends goes deeper than the distinction between liberal and vocational, and this is the distinction which is essential for a civilisation which has lost its way. The study of ends is to learn something, however little, of the meaning of life, and therefore of its purpose. To learn boxing, if boxing means a quicker eye and a cooler temper, may claim to be part of a liberal education, but it has nothing to say of Ends. Mathematics may train the powers of reasoning, and so belong to a liberal education, but it tells us nothing about life; it is an education in means, and not in ends. Theology, philosophy, history and literature, which tell of the nature of God and of the world, and of the achievements and visions of man, these are the four studies which deal with Ends. And even within them it is possible for a student to narrow his concern to means only. Research into the tactics of the Macedonian phalanx, or the rhythm of the *clausula* in Latin prose, may increase knowledge, and may be accounted part of a liberal education, but it is not to study Ends. If we are to have a national education which concerns itself with Ends, we shall have to take steps to see that as many as possible of our people receive some training in the broad elements of one, some, or all, of these four studies, theology, philosophy, history and literature. They need not necessarily be embarked upon before the age of fifteen, perhaps indeed they should not be, for a child has not the experience of life to profit much by a discussion of its meaning. But it is to be hoped that in a new age, in which the almost limitless powers of production will be better organised, so that we shall hear less of unemployment and more of leisure, there will be a huge development of adult education. But this at present lies beyond the immediate horizon, in the domain of what may be hoped, or resolved, but cannot as yet be achieved. It is not a change whose beginnings can grow out of the war itself, and so make us fitter to win it. Already, however, one essential part of the necessary change can be seen about to take shape in the contemporary scene.

§ 3

Since the Renaissance there have been two chief spiritual sources of British civilisation, Greece and Palestine. Let any one who doubts this consider the great figures of our past, and the influence of Palestine on Cromwell or Wesley, of Greece on Burke or Gibbon, of both on Milton or Gladstone. Of these two fertilising streams one, the Greek, has been allowed almost to dry up. Only an infinitesimal fraction of the young read Plato or Aristotle or Thucydides, even in translation. It may be that there is to be no second renaissance. Perhaps Greek literature will never be widely studied again in this country, even at second hand. Perhaps the Greek influence is now so generally and unconsciously assimilated that, though scholars and specialists will always turn back to its sources, the general public needs to know no more of it than is reflected in our own literature. Impossible to say. But that we ought to give far more of our citizens than ever before the foundations of an education in Ends, and that such an education cannot fail to include an introduction to philosophy or theology or history or literature, all of which have been profoundly influenced by Greek thought, this at least is certain.

The other spiritual source of our civilisation, however, is even now by no means lost to us. Our loss here has been progressive, though far from complete. Before the Reformation every peasant was familiar with the stories of the Saints, a storehouse of simple biography, ethics and theology, which provided a population which could not read with a rich traditional culture of its own. With the Reformation all this was lost; but after the Reformation there came in the almost universal habit of bible-reading, and there was the weekly sermon, and very often the daily prayers. Consider the close reality of the Old Testament to the Roundheads, of the New Testament to Wilberforce or Shaftesbury or Livingstone. These ages did not lack education in Ends. Among great masses of our population to-day, however, bible-reading and church-going are no more. In part we have become a civilisation of the cinema and the road house, cultureless and rootless. But only in part. Christian culture is very far from dead. And there are signs that it will revive, in the conflict. But how, and when and why?

§ 4

Clearly we are fighting against a pagan state. It is unnecessary, and, I think, injudicious, to paint Germany wholly black; a Germany which was wholly black indeed would be much less formidable than the reality. No doubt there are plenty of German virtues—if it comes to that, Satan himself, as Milton has reminded us, was a particularly splendid gentleman, possessing indeed almost all the virtues, except humility and a sense of humour. In spite of which he was the Prince of Darkness. No doubt, too, there are Christian churches, and countless sincere Christians, in Germany. None the less, the German state is pagan, and its victory would be the victory of paganism.

The evidence that the Nazi creed involves a frontal assault upon Christianity is overwhelming, and by now only too familiar. Typical samples of it are collected in *The Persecution of the Catholic Church in the Third Reich*. It is not merely that certain Nazi leaders have permitted themselves vulgar blasphemies against the Christian religion. Or that they have publicly proclaimed that Hitler has superseded Christ. Or that the official Nazi Schulungbrief treats Christianity as a disastrous interlude in the heroic history of Germany, and Rosenberg proclaims a new evangel, and new moral standards, according to which the Christian doctrine of universal love is "a blow at the heart of Nordic Europe," and "right and sacred," as the Gauleiter of Austria put it, "is . . . only what serves the nation and its preservation." Or indeed that a volume could be filled with the pagan utterances of Nazi protagonists. They have become wearisome by now, these Nordic blarings and bellowings. Much more significant than all this is the conflict between Nazi and

Christian which lies at the heart of Nazidom itself. Fundamental to Christianity is the doctrine of the equal and eternal significance of every human soul. Equally fundamental to Nazidom is the belief that human individuality is significant only as a contribution to the life of the state, so that the less fit may legitimately be exterminated, so that kindness to the weak is decadence, so that every departure from the official norm is treason, so that the ideal citizen is the warrior-ant. The Nazi idolatrously worships the state, as the Communist idolatrously worships humanity. The world-supremacy of such a state could not indeed finally extinguish Christianity, but clearly might drive it back to the catacombs for a thousand years. Is it possible that, since in two thousand years Christianity has not penetrated civilisation sufficiently to prevent civilisation from becoming what it is to-day, Christianity itself stands in need of such an experience. Kierkegaard, the Danish philosopher, prophesied a hundred years ago that Christianity would one day be taken from Europe, to teach Europe its value. We cannot rule out the ugly possibility. Once again the answer seems likely to depend upon whether or not we achieve regeneration through suffering, and in the course of the struggle conquer not only the enemy but ourselves.

§ 5

For though we are fighting against pagan forces, it does not follow that Britain itself can claim to be Christian. It is probably true that, seen from a distance, Britain is the country which most nearly approaches the ideal of a Christian community. It is true also that religion has always been interwoven with our public affairs. The Church of England is an established state church, and legally this is a Christian country. The ritual of the Coronation, the prayers which precede every sitting of either House, even the Mayor's chaplain all remind us that every degree of the hierarchy of Government is officially Christian. And the influence of religion, or at least of religious individuals, upon politics has been remarkable. Before the Reformation it was the Church which manned the administration. Since the Reformation, through Cromwell and the Puritans, Wilberforce and the Evangelicals who abolished the Slave Trade, Shaftesbury and the Factory Reformers, our increasingly democratic politics have maintained much the same tradition. It could be argued indeed that every politician in the last hundred years who has had a strong personal hold upon the masses has been a man of deep religious convictions. Certainly from John Bright and Gladstone to George Lansbury and Lord Halifax, the list would be an impressive one. Nor is this personal interrelation of politics and religion confined to national figures such as these. To this day, for example, it is remarkable how frequently the local Labour leader is prominent in Church or Chapel. Partly no doubt because it is the men of faith who are men of energy and courage. But partly also because the British public itself has always preferred a vein of religion in its leaders. Numerous—I almost said innumerable—religious and semi-religious organisations play their part in forming public opinion and influencing public policy. And although society is full of obvious injustices, the social services have been developed to a point at which they have been criticised by students of eugenics for deliberately promoting the survival of the least fit. Some say the motive was to avoid a social revolution, but in a very large measure it was the Christian instinct of kindness to the weak.

§6

All this, however, though it is evidence that there are plenty of Christian influences in the state, does not amount to justifying a claim that it is a Christian state, certainly not that it is a Christian state in anything remotely approaching the sense in which Germany is a Nazi state. The most reliable test, after all, of the religious stature of a people is its education. And this is a test which we can hardly hope to pass. The contrasting vices of sectarianism and apathy, which ravaged our educational policy in the opening years of this century, between them almost extinguished the serious teaching of religion in the state elementary schools. Religion became an "additional option" in the training for the teacher's Certificate, and in the schools was often taught by men or women who did not believe, and were not even interested, in it. It is not easy to imagine the Nazi creed being taught by apathetic or hostile instructors. This, of course, is not to say that there has not been much sincere and devoted teaching of religion in the state schools. But, making all allowance for the great variety in local practice in state schools, for the schools "provided" by various religious bodies, and for the private preparatory schools of the prosperous, as well as for the fact that the child's home, and the years which immediately follow school, may be more decisive influences than the school itself, it has to be admitted that up to the outbreak of war the elementary schools as a whole were turning out a formidable proportion of young pagans. The great migrations from the industrial areas in the first days of war revealed very large numbers of children who had scarcely heard the word "God," save as a swear-word. In one party, twenty-one children out of thirty had no notion why the feast of Christmas is kept. It is unlikely that there are many children in Germany who have heard of "Hitler" only as a conventional adjunct to "Heil," or who know nothing of the annual Party meeting at Nuremberg. In the secondary schools controlled by public authorities the same curious tradition, that it is improper to inquire of a would-be teacher, who may have to teach religion, whether he believes in it, had fairly widely established itself—as if Dr. Goebbels were to leave the opponents of the Nazi faith to instruct the young in its doctrines. As to the public schools, their traditional *ethos* is certainly Christian in origin and sentiment. If it had not been so they doubtless would not have provided us with our leaders for a century. As a writer in *Religion in Education* puts it:

" . . . we are fools if we do not recognise how largely public school morality is not only consistent with, but is derived from and is an exposition of, Christian faith. So far from affecting to despise it as something irrelevant to truly Christian education, we should thank God that there exist these corporate bodies in which

standards which, so far as they go, are Christian
standards are held up as those to which their members
are expected to conform."

Nurseries of sound character, no doubt, they still are, as
well as seminaries of more varied and lively learning
than ever before. But all this is another story. Christian
education, as distinct from education which derives
from Christian origins, or inherits Christian traditions,
is not education in a particular subject, but a particular
kind of education in all subjects. The Nazi school is not
a school which devotes an hour a week to teaching a
certain creed, but a school which teaches everything in a
certain way. And here it is noticeable that now and
again of late men have been appointed to the headmaster-
ships of great schools who, though undoubtedly virtuous,
idealistic and able, were not Christians, and as to whom
the Governors who appointed them, and this was the
significant novelty, did not care whether they were
Christians or not. And boys have been known to be
officially prepared for confirmation at a famous school
by a communist tutor, who frankly regarded all religious
belief as an antiquated and dangerous superstition. More
familiar, however, in the schools, as in the state, is the
virtuous agnostic, with the insidious distinction that in
the schools he still outwardly conforms.

In the Universities it is not necessary to conform.
Devotion to duty, the highest standards of personal
conduct, conscientious industry, the relentless pursuit
of truth—at the outbreak of war all these qualities were
probably more conspicuous in the Universities than ever
before. But once again, that is another story. Would
any one claim that of the teaching staffs of the Universities as a whole (the wealthiest and most ancient of

which are of course religious foundations) one half were practising members of any Christian denomination? Or one third? Or one quarter? And even clerical members of them would probably as often as not have agreed that it was not only irrelevant, but improper, to inquire, when appointing a colleague, perhaps to spend the rest of his life in intimate contact with the young, as to whether he regarded religion as the one means of salvation or as a particularly subtle form of poison. During this period there seemed nothing odd in appointing a University Reader in religion who believed neither in the divinity of Christ nor in personal immortality. And, to turn to the pinnacle of the system, whereas it would be impossible to hold the meanest public office in Nazi Germany without professing the Nazi creed, in Britain it would have been regarded as the last word in old-fashioned obscurantism to suggest that there was anything inappropriate in the spectacle (not unknown during the generation of the Armistice) of a Minister of Education who was an atheist. The place of Dr. Goebbels in the Nazi regime occupied by an anti-Nazi! It is clear that we cannot claim to be a Christian state in anything remotely approaching the sense in which Germany is a Nazi state. We are fighting against paganism; can it be said that we are fighting for Christianity?

§ 7

What we can at present claim to be defending is not Christianity, but Christendom; Christendom, a way of life which slowly took root in Europe during the age of faith. Democracy is not of course its only political expression, democracy indeed, even in this island, is a comparatively recent experiment, but democracy is the guise in which we of Western Europe have known Christendom for several generations. And the foundations at least of democracy are Christian. It was Christianity after all which, in an age of slavery and violence, first taught man the equal and eternal significance of every human soul, and, with all its faults, democracy may claim to be an attempt to embody that faith in the political structure. Very early in their history our forefathers boasted that an Englishman's home was his castle, and in the seventeenth century, by the Habeas Corpus Act of 1679, they finally succeeded in making it his castle. Henceforth, no man could be imprisoned without trial, because he had said, whispered, or even thought what was displeasing to a tyrant. Provided that he obeyed the public law, publicly agreed to by his elected representatives, his home was indeed his castle, within which generation after generation could be brought up through sheltered childhood to sturdy individuality. The Rule of Law had been established. And it is in the Rule of Law, even more than in the political mechanisms of ballot or Party, that the Christian tradition of freedom has expressed itself. Henceforth there were to be no secret police. And perhaps that is the most fundamental characteristic both of democracy and of Christendom; there are no secret police. In the years that followed, country after country reached the full stature of civilisation by following our example, and establishing the Rule of Law. It is only during our generation that, one by one, the lights have gone out in Europe, and the secret police have come back. In the last resort this war is the struggle to keep the secret police out of what is left of Christendom. Yet one more of Hitler's unpredictablt betrayals of his own unpredictable pledges has decreed that, for the present, this war to rid the world of the Gestapo should be fought in alliance with the Ogpu— even as we fought the last war, for democracy as we believed, in alliance with the police of the Russian Tsar. That does not alter, we cannot allow it to alter, what we are fighting for ourselves. Christendom: if its political basis is the liberty of the individual, freedom from the rule of the secret police, its moral character is dictated by the survival of the Christian virtues in an age which has largely abandoned the Christian faith. For of the virtues which Christianity taught mankind in the age of faith, the slow acquisition of which indeed itself constituted man's ascent from barbarism, many are still everywhere honoured, and indeed practised, even by those who have renounced, or have never known, the faith from which they once sprang. Nor is it merely a question of the survival of a state Church, the development of humanitarian social services, or the close association of religion, and religious organisations, with public affairs. The toughest young bruiser accepts instinctively, from the moral atmosphere he breathes, the assumption that he ought not to hit below the belt, or kick a man when he is down; the most cowardly egoist does not question the dictum Women and children first. We are by no means all honest, but we should all agree that a man's word ought to be his bond. Countless unreflecting citizens grow up with such well-worn popular maxims as these; to do so is their spiritual legacy from the past. But when once the faith from which the moral tradition sprang has vanished, a nation which continues to live by it has begun to consume its spiritual capital. With its roots withered or cut away the tradition itself cannot long survive. The rule of the virtuous agnostic is never more than a temporary phase. This is what Aristotle meant by saying that character could not be maintained without belief. Exposed as it is to-day to so formidable an offensive both from within and without, how can the moral heritage which is Christendom endure, unless its roots take hold again of their native soil?

"The traditional ideals of conduct in the medical profession are undoubtedly inspired by Christianity, those ideals which summon the individual doctor to put in the forefront of his mind not his own personal advancement but the unselfish service of humanity. But one cannot read such passages as the conversation between the newly qualified medical students in Sinclair Lewis' *Arrowsmith* without wondering how long a profession which cuts itself loose from its roots in Christian faith will be able to retain its Christian standards." [1]

Much the same might be said of many other kinds of human activity, including democracy itself. To quote the Master of Balliol:

"The doctrine of human equality has, of course, been affirmed and acted upon by men who have repudiated the religion which gave it birth—and, indeed, all religions. The belief can survive, for a time at least, what produced it. But it is a religious faith, and nothing but faith will maintain it." [2]

[1] Canon Leonard Hodgson, *What is meant by a Christian Education?*
[2] A. D. Lindsay, *I Believe in Democracy*, 13.

§ 8

If we are to construct again a civilisation conscious of Ends, we shall have to return to the sources of Christendom. It is surely the height of paradox to go through the fires in defence of Christendom, and yet deliberately to leave great numbers of our people ignorant as to what Christendom is. For that our present civilisation is the heritage of Christianity is agreed to-day even by writers, such as Professors Joad and Laski, who do not admit the truth of the Christian faith itself. Indeed under the revealing impact of war, a surprising number of observers are prepared to acknowledge that we are the heirs of Christianity, while continuing to protest defensively that they must themselves on no account be suspected of being Christians. Letters to the *New Statesman*, after an apologetic profession of personal orthodoxy, "I am certainly not a Christian, but . . .", proceed, in effect, to defend the Christian outlook.

> "I said . . . 'I think only Christ can save the world,' and he gave such a start of astonishment at such words coming from me that . . . But I want in this book to tell you what I mean by that astounding statement, and I hope you won't think I've got Buchmanism or Catholicism or anything 'religious' like that."

Thus Mrs. Leonora Eyles in *For My Enemy Daughter*, and the passage is characteristic of the sentiments of many writers who would not admit them so frankly. It is an odd, and probably a transitional, moral attitude, this attempt to make the best of both worlds. It is a curious intellectual position too, when you come to think of

it. The few months' ministry and preaching of an obscure
inhabitant of Palestine two thousand years ago has not
only won the allegiance of countless millions of ordinary
human beings, and inspired the lifework of innumerable
saints, martyrs, heroes and prophets, ever since, but is
admitted, even by its opponents, to condition the moral
atmosphere of what is left of civilisation to-day; and
yet the Individual who, with no human resources outside
Himself, was admittedly responsible for these unique and
prodigious consequences was Himself (as He must have
been, if He was not what He claimed to be) a deluded
self-deceiver upon a gigantic scale. Or, as Mr. C. S.
Lewis puts it:

"There was a man from among the Jews who
claimed to be, or to be the son of, or to be 'one with,'
the Something which is at once the awful haunter of
nature and the giver of the moral law. The claim is
so shocking—a paradox, and even a horror, which we
may easily be lulled into taking too lightly—that only
two views of this man are possible. Either He was a
raving lunatic of an unusually abominable type, or
else He was, and is, precisely what He said. There is
no middle way. If the records make the first hypothesis
unacceptable, you must submit to the second." [1]

"There is no middle way:" very many, however, nowadays
choose to imagine that there is a middle way, now that
the view, more characteristic of the self-satisfied nineteenth-century materialist, that the effects of Christianity
were positively harmful, is so largely abandoned. It is
a curious intellectual position, but, since it is fairly
common, it should mean that opposition to a revival of

[1] C. S. Lewis, *The Problem of Pain*, 11.

the study of the sources of Christian civilisation need not be virulent, as it might have been even a generation ago.

There is already a considerable movement making in this direction.

"There is an ever-deepening conviction that in this present struggle we are fighting to preserve those elements in human civilisation and in our own national tradition which owe their origin to Christian faith. Yet we find on every side profound ignorance of the Christian faith itself. There is evidently an urgent need to strengthen our foundations by securing that effective Christian education should be given in all schools. . . ."

That is a quotation from a statement issued from Lambeth in February, 1941, with the concurrence of the Free Churches. The actual proposals which the Archbishops proceed to sponsor are far from startling. In the secondary schools the recommendations of the Spens Report. In the elementary schools some religious instruction for all, except those whose parents wish them not to have it; and instruction by competent teachers. That is, in effect, what it amounts to. The modest nature of these proposals is evident enough if one substitutes arithmetic for Christianity. One has to imagine in the year 1941 a demand that, unless their parents happen to object to the subject, all children should be taught arithmetic, and that the lessons should be given by teachers who have learned the subject themselves. And one has to picture this suggestion requiring the organisation of a nation-wide campaign to back it, without any assurance, even so, of its overcoming in the immediate future the timidity and scepticism of politicians. Such have been the relative estimates, in our era, of the importance of arithmetic and religion.

All this, so far as it goes, is all very well. But it does not go very far. Christian teaching, as, if we needed reminding, the Nazis should by now have reminded us, does not mean giving a few optional lessons in a particular subject; it means teaching every subject in a particular way. There may have been something to be said in the Victorian era for the ideal of the completely undogmatic teacher, whose avowed aim was to stimulate an all-embracing scepticism in unreflecting and self-satisfied youth, fostering the notion that every one is entitled to his own truth, and that, in the last resort, one belief is probably no truer than another. But there is much less to be said for the pedagogy of the mentally sterilised in an age in which, as was said of Alexandria in the days of Clement, "ideas are abundant and serious convictions rare." "Choose for yourself; nothing is sufficiently certain to be worth taking on trust" was a valuable ideal when scientific inquiry was endeavouring to establish itself against superstition and obscurantism, and it is still a valuable introduction to the sciences. But just as the young can understand chemistry or mathematics, in a sense in which, simply because they lack the necessary experience, they can never understand history or literature, so it is a dangerous perversion to extend the ideal of scientific scepticism to the point of encouraging the schoolboy or the undergraduate to treat the accumulated wisdom of mankind as the scientist very properly treats its accumulated knowledge, doubting everything, and selecting and rejecting at will—if for no other reason than that schoolboys and undergraduates simply do not possess the experience on which to form a judgment worth having.

In the sphere of knowledge the scientist does, in practice, accept the conclusions of the past; he stands upon the shoulders of his predecessors. Why, in the sphere of wisdom, should the young be expected to rediscover painfully for themselves the moral and spiritual truths which the accumulated experience of past generations has accepted as making for a good life in individual and state? Even if it were nothing else, the traditional moral code would be a labour-saving device on the grand scale, saving those who accept it on trust from re-learning the age-old lessons by the painful and laborious process of making for themselves the age-old mistakes. I have already quoted[1] from a passage in Mr. Bertrand Russell's *Education and the Social Order*, in which he recommends temporary childless marriages for University students. His reasons are worth noting. It would enable them to work harder. "This," he says, "would afford a solution of the sexual urge . . . of such a nature that it need not take up time which ought to be given to work." This, of course, is precisely what it would not do. As an American doctor has observed, the suggestion that living with a girl need not take up much of an undergraduate's time is a ridiculous piece of academic sophistry. Once again, the Christian moral code is a labour-saving device on the grand scale. We are not bidden to live in that way because it is easier, but, in many ways at any rate, it *is* easier to live in that way, because to do so is in harmony with our real natures, because, in short, the world is made like that. All this argument, of course, is immensely rein-forced if you believe, as the Christian believes, in a body of eternal truth revealed to mankind in the life of Christ, and recorded in the New Testament.

Yet this ideal, of the teacher who does not teach, lingers

[1] See p. 45.

on in a good many plans for education in the new age. Mr. Francis Williams, for example, in *Democracy's Last Battle*, appears to believe that mankind has never yet known a proper system of education, because teachers have always endeavoured to instil some sort of belief into their pupils, instead of leaving them to choose their own. And yet it was precisely this vacuum in our schools, this refusal in certain subjects, and those of supreme import- ance to mankind, to teach *anything*, which presented the Nazis with their greatest opportunity. Confronted with rivals who taught nothing, those who taught *something*, however foolish and frantic, had no reason to feel inferior. It is surely possible, however, to recognise the full value of the ideal of scientific scepticism, and the full danger of its antithesis in the Nazi-Communist cult of the closed mind, and yet to realise that here too, as in so much else, it is our business to find a practicable mean between two dangerous extremes.

In particular in the higher forms of the public and secondary schools there ought to be teaching of religion at a more or less adult level. Many young men become agnostics simply because inevitably they find themselves comparing a childish knowledge of religion—what they learnt at their mother's knee, reinforced by a sketchy knowledge of the kings of Judah and Israel "got up" at school—with their adult knowledge of science or politics. And yet a moving and intellectually exciting book such as Mr. C. S. Lewis' *Problem of Pain*, far more modern than a science primer, is available to make the raw material of serious school lessons on religion and the problems of the modern world. Nowadays it is quite usual to find a well-read and intelligent writer treating the Christian faith with patronising superiority, much as a professor might speak of a virtuous but dull-witted

schoolboy, and then to realise from some chance phrase
that the writer supposes that the Darwinian theory of
evolution, or the fact that the condition of the world is
not what he would wish it to be, has once and for all
disposed of the claims of Christianity on intelligent
people. Such ignorance would scarcely be conceivable in
an educated country.

We have to reconstruct a civilisation conscious of Ends,
as well as of means; we shall only permanently maintain
Christendom if we return to the sources of Christendom.
These are two ways of saying the same thing. Moreover
we shall not find our way back to the sources of Christendom merely by insisting that children shall be given
Bible lessons, if their parents do not object. Education
in a Christian country can only mean a system in which
every educational institution possesses in some degree a
Christian background of its own, and this in turn can
only mean that a substantial proportion of the teachers
in it are Christians themselves. To-day even this ideal
may seem alarmingly difficult to attain, and it will
certainly astonish and enrage many. But then there are
many who do not desire that Britain should remain a
Christian country. That is a perfectly intelligible position,
but those who do desire that Britain should remain a
Christian country cannot aim at less than this. It cannot
be a question of rigid tests and official conformity. We
need the most competent teachers, whether they are
Christians or not (though even those who are not
Christians ought at least to be aware that to be intellectually justified in refusing Christianity involves disposing,
not merely of what one remembers of lessons at one's
mother's knee, but of St. Paul and St. Augustine, Aquinas
and Pascal, Newman and Kierkegaard): we also need a
proportion of Christian teachers sufficient to create a

Christian background to education. These are two apparently incompatible ideals, neither of which, however, should be pursued to the exclusion of the other. Somewhere between these two extremes a balance can be struck. As a writer in *Religion in Education* put it the other day, " to hold that religious considerations must never be allowed to weigh (in the selection of teachers) is as one-sidedly fanatical as to hold that they must always out-weigh all others." This is a compromise, but democracy lives by compromise. More than this might mean returning to some of the abuses which flourished before the abolition of religious tests. Less than this, and Christendom itself is doomed.

V

MECHANISM OF DEMOCRACY

§ 1

No Christian, nobody, indeed, who is conscious of a distinction between Ends and means, can believe that democracy is necessarily at all times and for all peoples the ideal form of political constitution. Nevertheless, believing in the ultimate significance of every human soul, the Christian—and, thanks to Christianity, many who are not Christians—will believe that any tolerable form of government must be one which permits the development of human individuality. And though in a democracy the sovereign majority may be tempted to iron out individuality and blanket the minority, a democracy is, in the nature of things, likely to make the free development of personality possible for a larger proportion of its citizens than any other political system. The autocracy of one of Plato's philosopher kings might well result in a civilisation more conscious of Ends, and a society more tolerant of the fullest expression of the individual self, than any other conceivable form of government; but unfortunately, with the doubtful exception of Marcus Aurelius, no omnipotent philosopher king has yet appeared in history. And, so far as humanity has gone, democracy at its best has come much nearer to combining the fullest development of individuality with order and government and the rule of law than any other constitutional experiment. We need not therefore spend much time here in discussing the relative value of British democracy as a constitutional form. Its weaknesses

106

are not inherent in its mechanism so much as in the uses
to which, human nature being what it is, its mechanism
is sometimes put. Nevertheless there are some reflections
which are worth while making upon the democratic
mechanism in the light of war.

§ 2

Most people who have reflected at all upon the nature of
democracy, and its relation to the age of the Blitzkrieg,
probably hold the opinion that the virtues of democracy
are chiefly moral, and best displayed in time of peace,
while its defects are mainly defects of organisation,
specially conspicuous in time of war. If this is so, it is a
flattering verdict, and we shall not wish to complain of it.

"The really precious things which democracy pre-
serves and cherishes are slow, and slowness is essential
to them—discussion and leisure, friendliness and kindli-
ness, decency and consideration and wisdom. None of
these can be hurried. They are not *blitz* qualities. . . .
It takes time to be a person: it takes time to treat other
people as persons. Good manners, which are the
outward expression of treating people as persons, take
time." [1]

It is true that the richest virtues (as well as some of the
worst defects) of a democratic society are not Blitzkrieg
qualities, and that they flower most fully and naturally
in peace-time. That indeed is why I have not discussed
them, or have discussed them only incidentally; for this
is not another treatise on British democracy, of which
there are plenty, but an attempt to survey our merits and

---

[1] *I Believe in Democracy*, by A. D. Lindsay, 58.

defects, as revealed in the harsh, unnatural light of the supreme test of war; an examination of our claim, thus tested, to survive, and, having survived, to create the new age. And yet is it wholly true that the merits of democracy at any rate, are not Blitzkrieg qualities? What of the tradition of friendliness, independence and enterprise nourished by the multitudinous voluntary associations of our democracy? Have not these played their part, and perhaps a decisive part, in withstanding the Blitzkrieg?

And there is a less obvious quality, lying on the border-line between politics and ethics, which surely makes for the survival of a democracy such as this in total warfare. Tradition, sentiment and conscience are all three powerful in our politics; indeed they are implicit in the Party system, for it is by these that men are held together in political association. The rulers of a totalitarian state, on the other hand, deliberately sterilise policy of such ingredients; nor is this cultivated cynicism by any means an innovation of the Nazi regime. Let any one who supposes *Mein Kampf* to be in this respect original, examine the eighth chapter in the first volume of Bismarck's *Gedenken und Erinnerungen*. Here he will find the essence of *Realpolitik* exposed in a long letter to von Gerlach, five years before Bismarck became Minister President, and more than seventy before Hitler became Chancellor. The heart of it is his insistence that when he decides on policy, *nothing* is to influence him, save the interests of Prussia; not tradition nor sentiment nor morality nor "stagnating antipathies," but *only* Prussian interests. It is the policy of the *tabula rasa*, the statesman's mind swept clear of every consideration save one. Now the cult of the *tabula rasa* is obviously impossible in a democracy. It is precisely tradition and sentiment and moral idealism that unite men in political Parties. In the

'eighties no British Liberal could begin to consider the
Eastern Question save in the light of Gladstone's Mid-
lothian campaign, and no British Conservative save in
the light of the Congress of Berlin and Disraeli's Crystal
Palace speech of 1872. But Real Politik meant that
Bismarck was free to be a Liberal, if he pleased, one year,
a Conservative the next, and both, or neither, in the third
—just as Hitler could pose as the great anti-Bolshevik,
the great pro-Bolshevik and the great anti-Bolshevik
once more in the space of less than two years. Now in
the age of Bismarck, in external affairs at any rate, Real
Politik appeared to be uniformly successful: but then the
age of Bismarck was probably the last in which it could
hope to be uniformly successful, for it was the last age
in which major wars were won by armies alone. To-day,
when great wars are struggles not between armies, but
between peoples, and all their moral and material resources,
it seems likely that the moral cynicism of Bismarck's
Real Politik, as adopted and adapted by Hitler, may prove
a fatal defect in his system. Bismarck could hand over the
Polish refugees to Russia in 1863, and ignore every
consideration save the advantages of ensuring Russian
neutrality in the coming war with Austria; it did not
matter to him that his policy might leave a streak of
rankling uneasiness in the nation's conscience, for the
nation was not going to be exposed to the moral stresses
of total warfare, under which an uneasy conscience may
mean an earlier collapse. It is not so with Hitler. His
treacherous onslaughts on Norway or Holland, the
astonishing *volte-faces* of his Russian policy—when the
last strain comes, and a people must summon its final
moral reserves, such memories as these, stirring uneasily
in the national consciousness, may well mean the difference between endurance and surrender. It is well for a

democracy that it is committed, by the very nature of its political system, to paying more regard than this to the moral susceptibilities of mankind.

§3

I began this chapter by saying that most people who have reflected on the nature of democracy, and its relation to the age of the Blitzkrieg, probably hold the opinion that the virtues of democracy are chiefly moral, and best displayed in time of peace, while its defects are mainly defects of organisation, specially conspicuous in time of war. And we have seen that the first half of this judgment needs some modification, since the virtues of democracy, although peace, doubtless, is the environment in which they flourish most fully, and for which they were, so to speak, intended, are also potent in total warfare. And indeed it would be strange if this were not so, since total war is likely, by its very nature, to make demands on every quality which a nation possesses. There remains the second half of the common judgment of democracy— that its defects are mainly defects of organisation, specially conspicuous in time of war.

Almost every one, I suppose, would agree that it is desirable, and in fact indispensable, that during a supreme national crisis there should, if possible, be a government representing all Parties in the state. The minority which objected so persistently to the National Government of 1931, objected because they held that it was not a real National Government, or that there was no real crisis; they did not argue that even if the nation were in real peril there ought to be no combination of Parties. Some democracies, it is true, have held this view, or, if they did not hold this view, have in fact failed to produce unity in the face of danger, and the most significant comment on them is that they are all defunct. When the existence of the state is threatened, the man in the street feels that it is intolerable that a considerable proportion of his elected representatives should devote their energies to opposing the Government. If this is what he feels, he is not entirely right. It is not intolerable that there should be Opposition, for the Parliamentary system is founded upon the assumption that Opposition is necessary to Government. What would be intolerable would be an Opposition which continued to act upon the too common assumption of Oppositions—that under all circumstances it is the duty of an Opposition to oppose. Even under a National Government, and during a crisis such as this, there will be some opposition, but it will come from supporters of the Government, who oppose because they genuinely believe that in this particular instance the Government is making a mistake, and not because they feel bound to act upon the assumption that it can never make anything else. The man in the street also feels that at a time like this the Government should be composed of the best talent available. Here, too, he is not entirely right. It would be difficult to maintain that the members of the present War Cabinet are the six or seven ablest men to be found in the two Houses of Parliament, let alone in the country as a whole. A National Government does not unite all the talents; it brings together the men who, through the Party organisations, command the confidence of the greatest possible number of Members of Parliament, and of the general public. Now though the reasons which he would give for feeling that at a time of crisis a National Government is both natural and indispensable may not be such as would commend them-

selves to a pedantic Parliamentarian, and though there
are a good many other reasons for the desirability of
a National Government which will not have occurred to
him at all, the fact remains that the instinct which bids
the man in the street demand unity in face of danger is
entirely sound; the history of Europe, indeed, is littered
with the wreckage of democracies in which the man in
the street either did not possess this instinct, or else was
unable to persuade his representatives to act upon it.

It was not, however, until after six months of the greatest
war in our history that we achieved in Britain a National
Government of all Parties. To be strictly accurate, it was
not even then an all-Party Government, for the Communists, represented by one Member of Parliament, did
not support it, continuing to profess the view adopted, by
49 votes to 9, in January, 1941, by the Annual Conference
of the University Labour Federation, that this was an
imperialist war—an attitude, however, not perhaps, as far
as the University Labour Federation was concerned, based
solely upon political considerations, since the *Daily
Worker* reported that certain undergraduates at Manchester
University were showing increasing opposition to the
war on the ground that it was "seriously interfering
with their studies."

Why was it not until the spring of 1940 that a comprehensive National Government at length came into
being, even in this country? Does this not point, it may
be said, to a radical defect in our political system? For
whatever the true explanation of that strange procrastina-
tion may be, it is surely at least no defence to say that
until the spring of 1940 it was believed that we were
fighting a "phoney" war. If Parliament had really
believed that a new war against Germany was not likely
to be among the most formidable episodes in our history,

such blindness would have been an even graver fault than the failure of the Parties to combine. Why, then, did it take us so long to form a National Government? Was some dangerous defect, some streak of unreality, in the Party system responsible, the same, perhaps, which accounted for the unedifying spectacle of the Opposition, on the eve of a war which it had already denounced the Government for not commencing in September, 1938, voting against conscription as recently as April, 1939?

But it may be said—in fact it has been said—that the Party system is in any case so self-stultifying, that in comparison with its permanent and inherent defects, its dilatoriness in achieving unity in face of danger is a mere peccadillo. Let us therefore for a moment cast an eye upon the Party system. I say the Party system, not the Parties, for here I am primarily concerned with the mechanism of democratic politics, and only secondarily with its beliefs. The creeds of all the political Parties happen to have been vitiated, as I hope to show in the next chapter, by certain illusions more or less common to all of them, but that fact does not decide the question whether or not it is desirable that government should be through Parties.

That the Party system is indispensable to Parliamentary Government is generally agreed—it was Disraeli who said, "I believe that without Party, Parliamentary Government is impossible"—so that, if it really is full of ineradicable defects, it must follow that Parliamentary Government, and therefore, presumably, democracy, in doomed. The Party tradition crystallised at a time when no unbridgable gulf divided the opposing factions. It was not merely, as is often cynically suggested, an artificial game of Ins and Outs. The political conflict between Walpole and Bolingbroke, between Fox and Pitt, represented two rival philosophies of life and politics. The practical issues on which they differed, too, were very great matters; Bolingbroke would have brought back the Stuarts, Fox would have sought an accommodation with Napoleon. Nevertheless it could always be assumed that the Parties agreed upon accepting certain common values, that they differed, so to speak, within a framework of agreement, that the Ins would not destroy the foundations of the State and that the Outs would not find it intolerable to live under the rule of the Ins. In the aggregate, revolutionary social and political changes have been brought about in the last hundred and twenty years, but they came one by one, and none of them quite seemed to be the end of the world to contemporaries. Moreover after the Reform Act of 1832, which opened the door to democracy, the Conservative leader, Sir Robert Peel, set the invaluable example of accepting the change, which he had resisted so strenuously, as a *fait accompli.* Since then, it would probably be fair to say that at any given moment something like eighty per cent of the politically conscious public has been in agreement upon the broad principles of domestic policy. Particular questions—the Corn Laws, Ireland or the Near East— have deeply, but transiently, divided men, but on the fundamentals of domestic policy they have almost always been in general agreement. And this has been so because at any given moment the mental climate was virtually all-pervasive. For the greater part of the last century, just as, with the steady succession of scientific discoveries and the steady growth of material riches, men were forgetting spiritual truths and falling victims to a pathetically self-satisfied materialism, so in politics they were all, in varying degrees, Individualists, believers in Laisser-faire and the economic survival of the fittest.

The Whigs were pre-eminently the Party of Individualism, as well as the traditional patrons of the insurgent middle classes, and therefore the Whigs were almost continuously in power for thirty years, but it would have been impossible to decide from a study of the statute-book alone whether in any particular year a Whig or a Tory Government was in power, for the simple reason that, with rare and unnoticed exceptions, both passed Individualist measures. A small tail of Radicals, loosly attached to the Whig Party, pressed for more rapid, more thoroughgoing and more doctrinaire Individualism than either Party, or the country as a whole, was prepared to accept. But otherwise the general harmony was only disturbed by occasional warnings from exceptional individuals, or small groups of enthusiasts—Coleridge, Carlyle, the Christian Socialists, the Owenites, the Young England Tories—to the effect that the doctrine of Laisser-faire was sterile and inadequate. But in the last quarter of the century, although in general a blind and self-satisfied materialism was still gaining ground, in the world of politics at any rate the mental climate was changing. By 1870 Individualism had shot its bolt. The doctrines of Bentham and Mill had been placed upon the statute-book, yet the expected Millennium had not arrived. Collectivism, the doctrine of state interference and state enterprise, began to take its place. Gladstone, who found the new doctrines meaningless or repellent, now inevitably found himself without a domestic policy, and turned his attention to Ireland or the Balkans. Disraeli, who had committed the Conservatives to Reform in 1867, committed them to Collectivism in his ministry of 1872-78, and left them in the ascendant for a quarter of a century. Mr. Lloyd George, with his new social services, brought the Liberals belatedly into line in the last years before the first German world war. By now the mental climate was Collectivist, and during, and after, the last war it became increasingly so. Liberal, and then Conservative, Governments placed a varied succession of Collectivist measures on the statute-book. Once again, from a mere inspection of the legislative output, it would have been impossible to deduce which Party was in power. Closely analogous to the Radicals of the last century, a small, but growing, tail of Socialists, loosely attached to the Labour Party (which became officially Socialist in 1918, but has always, in fact, been predominantly trade unionist), pressed for more rapid, more thoroughgoing and more doctrinaire Collectivism than either Party, or the country as a whole, was prepared to accept. But in general the mental climate of politics was so harmoniously Collectivist that a succession of Ins and Outs seemed as natural as in the eighteenth century. Whatever Party was in power, there would be expanding social services, electricity grids, Transport Boards and Broadcasting Corporations. True, a handful of prominent Socialists, exasperated by their crushing defeat in 1931, attempted for a while to popularise a very different conception of democracy, and determined that when, or if, a Socialist Government found itself in power, it would so "scramble the eggs," as Sir Stafford Cripps once put it, that they could never be unscrambled. This culinary operation was to be effected without the constitutional preliminary of consulting Parliament, through a civil service purged of insufficiently Socialist members, and Socialist District Commissioners superseding local authorities, on the Russian model, and, if necessary, by artificially prolonging the life of the Government, so that the electorate, which might possibly have developed a distaste for scrambled eggs, should not be able to express its opinions at a General

Election. All these remarkable intentions were professed in the writings or speeches of the well-known politicians and publicists who were prominent in a Socialist League which was the short-lived consequence of the electoral debacle of 1931. But the anti-democratic temper faded, as the events which had provoked it receded into the distance, and the menace of a genuine full-blooded anti-democracy began to loom upon the horizon of Germany. As to domestic controversy proper, even in the two years after 1931, though tempers rose high over the Means Test, the differences between the Parties remained differences of tone, temper and timing rather than of fundamental outlook. A certain number of the Government's critics who had lost their seats in Parliament did some harm to British prestige by touring the United States with the thesis that everything Britain did just now was selfish and obscurantist, but meanwhile at home the familiar succession of Collectivist measures—Passenger Transport boards, agricultural marketing boards, nationalisation of petroleum and the rest—was churned out by the legislative machine, and once again all you could have told from the statute-book was not that the Government belonged to any Party in particular, but only that it was Collectivist. In 1938 a well-known Member of the "Red" Clyde group once led by Messrs. Wheatley and Maxton, assured me that no important issues now divided the political Parties. All, in short, was as, more or less, it had ever been. The Outs were irritated by the Ins, and disapproved of them, but they could live comfortably enough under their rule; and there was every prospect that when in turn they became Ins themselves the same would prove to be true of the Outs-to-be. Thanks to an ingrained instinct for compromise, and against pushing any principle to its logical conclusion, the Party system worked. It ought

117

not to have worked, but it did. Between them, naturally enough, that instinct, and that system, make strongly for a hybrid economic structure. If ever the completely Socialist State were to arrive in this country, it would arrive, not at the stroke of a revolutionary pen on some apocalyptic Monday morning, but in so long a series of piecemeal measures, successively sponsored by so great a variety of politicians, that nobody would recognise it for a Socialist State when it appeared. Much more probably, however, the British Parliamentary system, itself but another expression of the fundamental illogicality of the British mind, will continue to reflect itself in an economic organisation which bravely attempts to make the best of both worlds, shunning alike the uncompromising Collectivism of pre-Stalinite Russia and the uncompromising Individualism of pre-Roosevelt America. Some industries will be nationalised, others will not; great tracts of the national life will be organised on the assumption that all men ought to be equal, but there will be considerable enclaves surviving on the contrary assumption that in some ways it is a good deal more interesting if they are not. Our social and economic life, like our political life, which to some extent directs their development, although not to so great an extent as all are directed by the indefinable ancestral genius of the nation, will continue illogical, hybrid, and eternally exasperating and unintelligible to all the pedants and ideology-mongers who believe that every particular should be deduced from one clear-cut *a priori* principle. Our social and economic life ought not to work, but it will. Unless we are defeated in this war, there will be no revolution on the Russian model, for the same reason that in the eighteenth century there was no revolution on the French model. And there was no French Revolution in Britain because the middle

classes, who seized power in France between 1789 and
1792, had been seizing power in England for five hundred
years. And there will be no revolution on the Russian
model because the working classes, who seized power, or
in whose name power was seized (whichever you prefer),
in Russia, in one year, have already been seizing it here
for fifty.

To put it in another way, Government in this country
has always been in the hands of men who knew where to
stop. No Government has either differed so violently
from the Opposition, or pushed its own doctrines to such
extremes, that it became intolerable for its opponents to
live under its rule. To quote Sir Alfred Zimmern:

"There is no conceivable constitutional specific against
civil war: the Americans, the French and the Swiss,
like the English, know this to their cost. But the best
of all safeguards against it is to cultivate a nice sense
of what ' can ' and what ' cannot be done ' in any
given circumstances—a sense which, in the world of
political practice, corresponds to the part played by
the conception of equity in the world of formal law." [1]

A country in which the Party in power has not known
where to stop, so that to its opponents anything seems
preferable to its continuation in power, is necessarily
doomed, since it is incapable of cohesion even in face of
the most deadly danger. In such a country the most
powerful Parties, and perhaps all Parties, will behave as
the diminutive Communist organisation in Britain
behaved. But that, fortunately, is not our fate.

[1] *From the British Empire to the British Commonwealth*, 12.

§4

Very well, then, the Party system itself is not, as some have maintained, so self-stultifying that it is a barrier to all effective action, so self-stultifying that, in comparison with its permanent and inherent defects, some dilatoriness in achieving unity in face of danger is a mere peccadillo. On the contrary, it wears every appearance of being the indispensable condition of progress without revolution. At any rate this seems to be true of the Party system in relation to domestic policy. It is not so clear that it is true with regard to foreign policy. And here I shall unhesitatingly refrain from treading yet once more the well-worn path of retrospective controversy, of acrid wisdom-after-the-event, which leads from the Treaty of Versailles to September the third, 1939. Not that it is not tempting to do so; it is easy enough to make fun of anybody who committed himself to any brand of foreign policy between 1919 and 1939, including oneself. A memorable anthology might be published, heart-wringing or rib-tickling according to taste, of pronouncements on foreign policy by every shade and variety of politician and publicist. But its publication would do nobody much good to-day, particularly if, as is, I am afraid, only too probable, the miscalculations of only one genus of politician were included. Nevertheless, in general terms at least, it is necessary to ask, Is the Party system necessarily self-stultifying in the domain of foreign policy? May not a domestic policy of compromise, and a hybrid economic structure, be one thing, and a diplomacy of compromise something very different, and very much more dangerous?

There can be no doubt that compromise, and indeed

contradiction, is written large over the whole sequence of our foreign policy during the twenty-one years' armistice. Perhaps compromise and self-contradiction were inevitable, in an age of fanatical ideologies, for the British with their "unfanatical handling of fanatical conceptions," and their easy combination of ideals found on either side of the political battlegrounds of Europe. Compromise and self-contradiction there certainly was, and some of it, it is to be feared, was inherent, not so much in our mentality as in our political system. To have dealt from the outset, and to have continued to deal, so sternly with Germany that she would never be able to lift a hand against the peace of Europe, this, as Hitler's own programme for victory has since reminded us, would have been a perfectly possible, as well as a perfectly intelligible, policy. It would not have come easily to us; to a majority of the nation, with its humane instinct for letting bygones be bygones, it would have seemed unnatural and even immoral; but it is possible that it might have succeeded, and now in retrospect we can at least imagine ourselves pursuing it. On the other hand, to have dealt so generously and leniently with Germany that she would never again wish to lift a hand against the peace of Europe, this also would have been a perfectly possible, and a perfectly intelligible, policy. It would have come easily to us—in the tradition of the "gentlemanly" terms accorded to defeated France after the Napoleonic wars, thanks to the influence of a few English aristocrats at the Congress of Vienna, in the tradition, too, of the generous treatment of the Dutch Republics after the South African War. Right or wrong, it was, I think, our first instinct, and certainly the first instinct of our fighting men; on the day on which the terms of the Versailles Treaty were known, a protest against their harshness was drawn up and signed by most of the ex-servicemen in the University of Oxford. It is possible that such a policy might have succeeded, and in retrospect we can at least imagine ourselves attempting it. Perhaps indeed, if we had been left to ourselves, if it had not been for Clemenceau and the French, we should actually have given it a trial. In fact, however, we compromised, attempting to pursue both policies, and in consequence inevitably reaping the disadvantages of both, and the advantages of neither. It was an epoch in which we could make friends of neither Communist Russia nor Fascist Italy, in which we allowed the French to dissuade us from countenancing the economic union of Germany with Austria, but ourselves persuaded the French to sit still when Hitler re-militarised the Rhineland. We had enraged Germany, but had not overawed her. We suffered all the disadvantages of being armed, together with all the disadvantages of being disarmed.

There is little to choose between the records of the Parties. The Conservatives, however, as the Party which exercised most power, and exercised it at most, though not all, of the decisive moments, will probably, at the assize of history, be required to shoulder most of the blame. Here, too, we see the true pith and nature of Conservatism eaten away by compromise. By the time that storm-clouds had begun to gather on the horizon it is more than likely that the deep instinct of the leading Conservatives (and in England at least Conservatives have long been a permanent majority of all classes) made secretly for the old-fashioned specific of armaments and alliances. But the deep instinct of Conservatives was never allowed to express itself. For a generation they had been paralysed and bewildered by a tradition of deference to their political opponents which had partly resulted in, and in part was itself the result of, a deep-seated sense of intellectual inferiority. For a generation they had derived the substance of their consistently Collectivist domestic programme from Socialist textbooks. In an age whose mental climate was ubiquitously Collectivist, this was inevitable and indeed salutary, but it did not make either for independent thinking by Conservatives, or for their confidence in their own traditions or instincts. In the Press, moreover, they had tamely surrendered the literary, artistic and intellectual movements of the time to their opponents. They were hardly in a condition to stand out against the currents fashionable in foreign policy. And these made strongly against armaments, and in favour of the League of Nations. Mr. H. G. Wells had called the fortification of Singapore "a monstrously stupid crime," "a frank provocation to crippled and devastated Japan." [1] And as late as 1935 Sir Herbert (now Viscount) Samuel, as leader of the Liberal Opposition, had declared, quite truly, that:

. "The powerful peace movement in this country has been vehemently opposed to increases in armaments, and the government are aware of that fact. . . . Branches of the League of Nations Union, the Churches, women's organisations and members of all Parties feel most deeply that . . . disarmament is essential as a means to peace. The Government, faced by that feeling, desire to turn it round the other way and would wish that all that sentiment . . . shall acquiesce in . . . increases of armaments for the sake of fulfilling, as they say, international obligations." [2]

[1] H. G. Wells, *A Year of Prophesying*, 23.
[2] House of Commons, March 11, 1935.

Against rearmament clamoured many other respected figures, many of whom have since bitterly denounced Lord Baldwin and his Government for not rearming swiftly enough. At this time (1935), it should be noted, the Navy's capital ships had been reduced, since 1914, from sixty-nine to fifteen, and its cruisers from a hundred and five to fifty, the Air Force had decreased from 3,300 first-line aeroplanes in 1918 to 850 in 1934, at which point the Government, despite a vote of censure by the Opposition, began slowly to increase them. The Government was doubtless to blame for the tardiness of our rearmament, since it was the Government. Only, if any one is entitled to blame the Governments of that time, it is not the Opposition, which still regarded the League of Nations as a safer and more agreeable alternative to armaments. The Government, though it did not share this view, lacked the courage to denounce it.

The danger of the League was, of course, that, dominated by the beneficiaries of the treaties of 1918, with the naturally conservative Titulescu of Rumania and Benes of Czechoslovakia ever influential, it came to represent a static ideal, and though constantly concerning itself with the problem of how to organise collective resistance to aggression, had done nothing to make aggression unlikely by providing machinery for peaceful change. It was thus that, although in this country tens of thousands of fervent peace lovers continued to revere the League with an all but religious enthusiasm, it eventually became one of the principal obstacles to lasting peace.

It had rendered an eventual explosion almost inevitable, while continuing to nourish in its devotees an illusory sense of security; surely, they felt, there was safety in numbers, surely so much genuine idealism could not be destined to run to waste? Only at the very last and with great reluctance did those who had built their hopes on Collective Security come to acknowledge the truth, at that time at any rate, of Professor Namier's aphorism, "Those who are interested cannot be impartial, and those who are not interested cannot be effective. How, then, can you have international action?" And meanwhile in this country an active and influential League of Nations Union powerfully disseminated just that combination of genuine idealism, "progressive" atmosphere, wishful thinking, and mental confusion which the Conservativism of the 'thirties was intellectually and morally least qualified to resist. A somewhat disingenuously entitled Peace Ballot, which came near to inviting its signatories to testify merely that they preferred peace to war, over-shadowed the election of 1935, at which Lord Baldwin was engaged on inviting the nation to approve the long-delayed and far from whole-hearted beginnings of re-armament. The state of mind of a good many of those who had added their signatures to the Ballot was typified by a constituent who wrote to the Government candidate in the course of this election that what he personally desired was a sound League of Nations policy, which he had always understood to mean no commitments abroad, and no expenditure on armaments at home. Towards the whole complex of aspirations and opinions embodied in the League of Nations Union and the Peace Ballot the Conservatives on the whole conducted themselves with a sort of deferential scepticism. They did not whole-heartedly approve, but they did not whole-heartedly denounce. They accepted the policy of the Union, but with crippling mental reservations, and they accepted it, moreover, without the one essential correction which they were themselves specially qualified to add to it.

They did not effectively rearm. All the good will and idealism which centred on the League of Nations, and even more obviously perhaps on the League of Nations Union, in the 'twenties and 'thirties, might perhaps have been canalised and concentrated into an effective foreign policy by a Government which itself profoundly believed in the League, and was prepared both to accumulate the armaments and to educate opinion up to the dangerous responsibilities which a thoroughgoing League policy must entail. Such a Government would presumably have been prepared to fight, and would have led the nation to be prepared to fight, a League war over Manchuria, as well as (if the later crises had arisen) over Abyssinia and Czechoslovakia. And "prepared to fight" implies both readiness of mind and spirit, and readiness of material resources. Such a Government, therefore, would presumably have armed Britain to the teeth, while sparing no pains to educate British opinion up to the shocking responsibilities of being the chief, and possibly the only, power prepared to fight the battles of Collective Security all over the terrestrial globe. Such, one must suppose, would have been the policy of a Government which profoundly believed in the League.

But the Government did not profoundly believe in the League. It saw the contradictions and dangers in the League's mixture of idealism and self-interest, in its commitments all over the world, in the reluctance or inability of most of its members to fight, clearly enough to be unable to prepare for, and pursue, a League policy at all costs, while remaining too deferential towards all the League of Nations Union stood for to sponsor the alternative, which many of its supporters would secretly have preferred, of an "old-fashioned" heavily armed defensive alliance. Not long before Hitler entered

Vienna, Mussolini had invited Blum, then in office at the head of the French *Fronte Populaire*, to co-operate to save both Czechoslovakia and Austria. Blum refused, and, with the League already a broken reed, the last slender chance of averting war by the only alternative to the League had finally disappeared. Their suspicion of the radical unsoundness of France under the *Fronte Populaire*, in which they judged more shrewdly than their Liberal and Labour critics, added its quota to the constitutional inability of British Conservatives to effect the diplomatic revolution which many of them must have secretly yearned for, and stake all upon a reversion to "the old diplomacy." Yes, I am afraid that it must be admitted that British foreign policy between the two world wars was fatally instinct with compromise, and that compromise, which may succeed in making the best of both worlds at home, is more likely to mean the worst of them abroad. Does it follow, then, that the Party system stands condemned, so to speak, upon the threshold of any inquiry, that it matters little whether or not it is capable of concentrating the united energies of the nation in times of danger, since it is in any case only too likely to have been itself the chief source of the very danger which it will eventually be called upon to resist? I do not think that this need necessarily be our conclusion. May not the errors of our diplomacy have been due less to a compromise between two clear-cut alternatives than to a defect common to both of them?

In its own way the policy of the Liberal and Labour Parties was equally contradictory, although, since they were in a permanent minority, their official responsibility was much less. It might have been possible to say that they represented the clear-cut alternative of a logical and whole-hearted League diplomacy, were it not for the fatal inner contradiction that they first backed our single-handed disarmament, and later resisted our belated re-armament, to the last perilous moment. They were in favour of a Continental policy, but against the only possible means by which it could have been carried out. The Labour Party, indeed, was virtually pacifist as recently as 1935, in which year it won a bye-election on the cry "armaments mean war," and then published a programme for the general election warning the electorate that "more guns . . . mean still dearer food." Long after this date it voted against armaments, and as lately as April, 1939, against conscription. As recently as the early months of 1941 Lord Cecil, in *A Great Experiment*, could make his chief charge against British policy the complaint that we did not disarm even more completely. Indeed even now, to judge from his autobiography, Lord Cecil has learnt nothing and forgotten nothing. His recipe for world security after the war is a confederation of those states which "fully accept the principle that aggression is an international crime and are prepared to use all their strength to protect victims of it." It has not, apparently, occurred to him that it too often happens that those who think aggression a crime have no strength, while those who have strength think that there is a good deal to be said for aggression. If he again discerns a country which is both strong and unaggressive, will Lord Cecil's policy again be to disarm it, and then to abuse it for not having disarmed more completely?

To clamour that, on behalf of the League, Britain should take a strong line with Japan over Manchuria, with Italy over Abyssinia or with Germany over Czechoslovakia cannot be said to have amounted to an alternative policy, since the advocates of the strong line had never insisted on rearmament, had indeed energetically opposed it. To argue, as some of them did argue, that mere bluff would have been sufficient, that any or all of the Axis powers would have executed a humiliating withdrawal in face of a few resolute gestures by a power which they knew to be spiritually and materially unprepared for war, was merely evidence of the sort of irresponsibility which may (or may not) be pardonable in an Opposition, but is certainly not permissible to a Government. The fundamental fact remains that the Opposition, too, had done nothing to prepare the nation for the wars which it was so often anxious that the nation should risk. Indeed it had done a good deal to ensure that the nation was not prepared. Not only were the tanks and aeroplanes not ready; the people had been deliberately encouraged to suppose that, provided they believed in the League, subscribed to Peace Ballots, and relied on Collective Security, there would be no need to fight. They could have, in short, the best of both worlds. They could continue to enjoy the highest standard of living in Europe, without rearmament and without conscription. They could remain prosperous and powerful without making sacrifices. They could have the best of all butter, but no guns. As the Foreign Secretary put it the other day—less bluntly, as becomes a Foreign Secretary, but not so very much less bluntly:

"We had believed, perhaps too easily, that a peace system that would recommend itself to the good sense of all peoples could be planned and debated in the council-room without other effort and without harder sacrifice on our part. We have learnt that this is not so; that the price of peace is constant vigilance, readiness, courage; and we must never forget that lesson.

The sacrifices of peace-time, necessary to guard against the ever-recurring danger of war, are hard, but they may be hardening and salutary." [1]

The most dangerous temptation of democracy during the last hundred years has been to make material comfort its chief goal and ideal, and to fear hardship and sacrifice like the plague. Mr. John L. Lewis, the American Labour leader, told the American Youth Congress, "I want the young men and women of America to *dream* about the day when they will have a job that will enable them to live in comfort and security," and Mr. Gaynor Maddox has recorded how a boy wrote to him a comment on this definition of idealism, "That is all we want. The draft (conscription) will upset the country, and make us young fellow slaves. It's a plot to keep us from getting what we have a right to." It was the members of the American Youth Congress who, in 1938, denounced Mr. Chamberlain as an appeaser, and in 1941 paraded Pennsylvania Avenue singing, "No, Major. No, Major. We will *not* go. We'll wager, we'll wager, this ain't our show."

Beside the fundamental and all-embracing illusion that peace, power and prosperity could be preserved without self-sacrifice, the other more particular and local illusions of the Opposition—the belief that Soviet Russia, which by 1939 had fought twelve wars of aggression, was an unselfish lover of peace at any price, the belief that the tyranny of the secret police, vile when exercised by a Gestapo, becomes mysteriously consistent with personal liberty when exercised by an Ogpu, the lively sympathy for the martyrdom of Pastor Niemöller coexisting with complete indifference to the martyrdom of his fellow-

[1] Mr. Anthony Eden, speech to Foreign Press Association, July 29, 1941.

Christians in Spain or Russia—all these appear as no more than short-sighted but almost amiable personal prejudices. The brief climax, at Munich, illumined the whole tragicomedy in one epitomising flash. The appeasers (including myself) had altogether underestimated the grim and treacherous scope of Nazi ambition, wishfully supposing that they were witnessing the last of a series of changes in the map of Europe effected, since the League had provided no alternative formula, by the doubtless clumsy, immoral and dangerous method of threat of violence, and each successively approaching nearer to the dreaded border-line, yet never, even in the breathless week of Munich, actually crossing it. And now all was to be well. Somehow, without arms, we had muddled through. The enemies of appeasement, on the other hand, had altogether misunderstood the part played by France, supposing that the French, who, unlike ourselves, were allied to Czechoslovakia and indeed in the Czechs were sacrificing their entire European system, would have been prepared to fight, had it not been for British poltroonery, and maintaining, once again, that, with Britain still notoriously unarmed, one final piece of bluff by Mr. Chamberlain would have brought Hitler to his knees. In the last resort it was not compromise which made our diplomacy impotent, it was our collective persistence in living in a world of unrealities, the deliberate nourishing of the illusion that we could continue to be great without sacrifice, that seated upon a heap of riches, and trusting to a minimum of weapons and a maximum of bluff and good fortune, we possessed a mysterious title to survive unscathed amidst a ring of ravenous and powerful rivals. The Party system will undoubtedly make for a diplomacy of compromise, at any rate in an era such as that which we have just passed through, in which there

are sharply divided views, and the predominant Party
is less whole-heartedly in harmony than its opponents
with the mental climate of the time: if the Opposition
Parties had been in power, be it noted, there might, or
might not, have been a more successful foreign policy,
but there would almost certainly have been less compromise.

All the same, though our foreign policy may have been
a compromise, and compromise may ultimately have
meant disaster, in the last resort we have to remember
that this compromise between conflicting views was
sustained and justified by one fundamental harmony.
All Parties wanted peace. A gifted and impartial observer
in the United States, surveying our contradictions and
hesitations during the last twenty years, summarily
dismisses two once fashionable explanations—the thesis
of some Communists and Socialists (once useful in
domestic controversy, though not perhaps even then
very deeply believed even by its sponsors) that Mr.
Chamberlain, Lord Halifax and a " Cliveden set " favoured
Fascist aggression in order to further a reactionary policy
at home, with the contrary thesis of the Nazis themselves
that, fearing the disintegration of her Empire, Britain
deliberately courted enmities, so that pressure from
without might strengthen the cohesion within. Mr.
Albert Viton preferred his own conclusion:

"Years of observation from front-row seats have
convinced me that motives totally different from those
commonly attributed to them swayed British statesmen. I am convinced, in brief, that a sincere and deep-
rooted hatred of war and fear of the ultimate consequences to Western civilisation—and the Empire—
of a world-wide slaughter were far more powerful

factors in shaping British policy. . . . So strong was the reaction in Britain against all the policies and ideas and practices which had led to the colossal massacre of 1914-1918 that the quest for peace was, on the whole, the mainspring of policy." [1]

And in diplomacy even compromise is less perilous for a great nation than the basic illusion that this time it is to be let off more lightly than the rest of mankind, that, for once in a way, the laws of destiny are to be suspended in its favour. Moreover the danger of compromise is not likely, as we shall see later on, to be so formidable to our diplomacy when this war is over. But the illusion that we can have security without sacrifice, the temptation in an age of materialism to put comfort first, the proneness of politicians to harp on rights and underestimate the people's capacity to remember duties, these are propensities which will be always with us, unless we are purged of them in the struggle. In the next chapter I shall discuss the prospect that this may prove to be a part of our regeneration.

§ 5

The Party system, it must be admitted, was not seen at its best in the diplomacy of the last ten years. But then the last ten years were a uniquely exacting test. War, of an unprecedented and frightful character, war as a result of which the public had long been encouraged to expect an end, and not a rebirth, of civilisation, loomed ever nearer. And humanity can hardly be expected to behave with unruffled wisdom in such a predicament. It is not necessary for a democrat to believe that the common

[1] Albert Viton, *Great Britain*, 222-3.

man in his millions is the best judge of every transient phase of a complex international crisis. Indeed democracy does not expect the masses to pronounce judgment upon particular issues at all. In an age hag-ridden by increasingly intricate problems these are usually best left to the experts. What the democrat should believe is that on broad moral issues the common man in his millions will judge better than any panel of experts which could be assembled. It is in the general election, in fact, that the people as a whole exercises its true function. And general elections increasingly assume the character of an appeal for "a doctor's mandate;" which means not so much a decision upon some highly complex problem, such as the gold standard—on which the ordinary man cannot expect to possess the knowledge to form an adequate judgment—as a choice between two, or possible three, alternative leaders, and the contrasting impressions which they contrive to convey of the sort of policy which, if circumstances permit, they are likely to pursue during the next few years. On such a broad issue as this I do not doubt that, in this country at any rate, with its long political experience, the common man in his millions does in fact judge more wisely than any conceivable oligarchy of experts.

This, I think, was more or less what Mr. George Glasgow had in mind when he wrote:

"These hard intellectuals whose vision is bounded by what their material brain opens to them do not, in fact, see far. In the life of man unexpectedness is the manifest means to an ordered plan. The pure intellectual is nearly always wrong in his judgment of future probability, no matter how deeply fortified his judgment may be by knowledge of worldly facts. There are tramps, who read no books, whose interpretation of what is at present taking place rings truer than that of learned people." [1]

It would not be difficult to argue that at every general election during the last century, with the possible exception of the "khaki" elections which capitalised war passions in 1901 and 1918, the wisest choice possible was in fact made by the electorate.

But it is a dangerous misconception of the democratic faith to encourage the masses to be continually passing judgment upon particular problems, or the transient phases of a prolonged crisis. This is a perversion which has been carried a good deal further in the United States than in this country. Gallup polls, straw votes and other test samples of public opinion may be very useful as a means of discovering the latent discontent which is evidence of administrative failure—the public wears the shoe provided for it by its rulers and only the wearer knows where the shoe pinches—but treated, as they seem to be treated in the United States, as an almost day-to-day guide, or corrective, for high policy, they imply a misconception of the whole nature of democracy which may prove disastrous. No society which substitutes mass observation for leadership could endure for long. It is only when confronted with the full responsibility of actual decision on a great issue, disencumbered of complex details and transient irrelevances, that humanity in the mass can be trusted to be wise. And this is specially true of the supremely difficult decision between peace and war. All moral action has been said to depend upon choosing a greater but more distant, in preference to a nearer but lesser, good, and the choice between war and peace is an

[1] *Diplomacy and God*, 179.

outstanding example of that truth. When the issue is presented to it fairly and finally, a democracy can be relied on to prefer a righteous war to an unrighteous peace, or to follow leaders who make that choice for it; but it will cut a much less impressive figure if its political temperature is taken every week or two by self-appointed observers, and if its leaders constantly regulate their policy by this fever-chart, instead of waiting to turn to the people at the crucial moment and for the final sanction.

§6

On the whole, then, the Party system is sound. Its inevitable, and, on the whole, invaluable, by-product, compromise, may sometimes muddy and deflect foreign policy, but there, we saw, the chief shortcomings were due to the reluctance of all Parties to invite the nation to face sacrifices in peace-time. Naturally the Party system has other defects. In particular, it is much too apt to prevent Parliament, or at any rate the House of Commons, from concerning itself with problems and proposals which do not figure on the Party programmes. And such matters are often of much greater moment than those which possess, for politicians, the merit of arousing zestful Party controversy. The road casualties, for example, regularly over a hundred thousand a year, interested the Commons very little indeed; they had not entered the domain of political controversy. Yet they represented a social evil, and an aggregate of human suffering, far more formidable than a dozen questions to which the House of Commons has devoted hours of discussion over many years, and perhaps as formidable as the problem of unemployment itself, which convulsed politics for a generation. In the same way even to-day there are probably plenty of serious hardships and grievances never aired in Parliament, simply because it would not be to anybody's electoral advantage to take an interest in them. For normally a new problem, not vouched for by a Party machine, can only gatecrash the arena of legislative action when it has already become acute, and probably dangerous. It has been calculated that on the average nineteen years elapse between the findings of a Royal Commission or Select Committee and the legislative action which follows it, and Sir Alfred Zimmern has pointed out[1] that it did in fact take us precisely nineteen years to recognise the menace of air warfare to our island security. But all these defects are just now relatively unimportant. The supreme merit of the Party system, the sovereign proof of its vitality, is that it can still be relied upon to produce unity in times of danger. Why, then, we must ask again, that six months' interval between the outbreak of war and the birth of a National Government? There were no doubt subsidiary reasons, but the chief reason, I am afraid, was that where principles no longer hold Parties apart, personalities often will. Jealousies, grudges, long-remembered slights, and the mere inexplicable dislike of one individual for another—I do not like thee, Dr. Fell—it is inevitable that all these should mingle inextricably with more creditable passions in any field of activity where men work, and compete, together; but there is undoubtedly something in the whole nature and organisation of Parliamentary life which makes it specially susceptible to personalities. And it was probably the presence in the Government of certain individuals whom the Opposition disliked and distrusted, more than any quarrel with its principles,

[1] *Spiritual Values and World Affairs*, 35.

which kept the two apart. Even a National Government is an all-Party, not a non-Party, combination and inherits the personal vendettas of its constituent elements. How else, for example, can the relegation to Canada early in 1941 of Mr. Malcolm MacDonald be explained—a superlative public servant, one of the two or three ablest Ministers, and one of the very few representatives among them of the missing generation, who had won golden opinions from every qualified judge of his work in each office he had filled, but whose name could not be forgiven him by some of his father's enemies? It is one of the merits, however, of a National Government that in general it is an effective solvent of personal enmities, just as in general it is one of the special virtues of British public life that it breeds much fewer, and far less remorseless, personal feuds than have politics in almost every other country. For years Mr. Churchill was the *bête noire* of the Labour Party; this indeed is how the *New Statesman* described him in 1931—when he was already agitating for more armaments.

"His mind . . . is confined in a militaristic mould; as a young man he learned to see everything in terms of war and preparation for war. There is perhaps not much you can do with this kind of mentality. . . . But Mr. Churchill, whom one used to fancy as an exuberant and stimulating person, hates youth and its idealism . . . he lives deep in the Victorian age, with his mind in ancient ruts about (*sic*) competition and Empire and Balances of Power. He is the oldest old woman in Europe." [1]

To-day Mr. Churchill counts some of his most enthusiastic supporters among members of the Labour Party.

[1] *New Statesman*, July 4, 1931.

§7

We may safely conclude, then, that a comprehensive and effective National Government has been the principal contribution of the Parliamentary system to the present struggle. And it follows as certainly, I think, that a National Government of the same calibre will be essential as far as we can see ahead, even into the years after the end of the war. A small minority of ideologues will undoubtedly maintain, very soon after the last bomb has fallen, that our political divisions are once again too deep for further cohesion. Have I not, only the other day, heard a University don exclaim with passionate nostalgia that what we shall most need after the war will be the leadership of Messrs. Laski and Gollancz? But the vast majority of the nation will be only too thankful to see co-operation continued, and in fact not only, as I have remarked already, was there no sundering gulf of principle between the Parties before the outbreak of war, but the first stages of post-war reconstruction will prove to have been dictated by measures to which we have already committed ourselves in war-time, so that they are unlikely to raise serious divisions in time of peace. There should be plenty of open Parliamentary criticism, once the war is over, but this does not necessarily mean that there need be a formal Opposition. Criticism of a government's measures from those who are in general its supporters can be more effective than criticism from those who feel bound to criticise, because they are the Opposition. Speeches, under these conditions, might even turn votes, so that the tedious formality of debates whose result is a foregone conclusion might gradually be outgrown. It will not be easy to maintain

National Government, even if we wish to; the social appetites which make for disruption are always powerful, and there are many individuals and organisations with what may be called a vested interest in Party conflict. The tendencies which make for the obliteration of Party should not, however, be underestimated. It is not merely that the flood itself will have effaced most of the old landmarks. Long before the war many of the most politically conscious minds found themselves moving outside, and away from, Party boundaries. The sponsors of the broadsheet *Planning* thus described, in 1935, the frame of mind which set their investigations going:

> "We were struck by the futility of all the old Party cries in the face of huge new problems whose solution called not for pigheaded partisanship but for a spirit of give-and-take, an eagerness to change one's point of view in the light of new information, and an unwarping adaptability to fresh ideas and fresh situations too numerous and too complex to be fully foreseen. . . ." [1]

And of the impartial, quasi-scientific approach to the complex and technical problems, which make up so much of modern politics, they wrote:

> "It is an approach exceedingly unpalatable to the partisan-minded, who like to take their ideas in neat antitheses of heaven and hell, black and white, or Left and Right. In fact, the born partisan and the seeker after magic remedies find something shocking and almost incomprehensible in such an organised effort to discuss facts in an objective and exploratory

[1] *Planning*, Jan. 1, 1935.

spirit. On the other hand, we have been encouraged to know that the growing element of scientifically minded people and the still important element who are guided rather by intuition and common sense than by any logical and hard-and-fast political orientation find in this approach a realism and an adaptability which the political Parties from their nature cannot give. . . . Political Parties remain, and must remain, essential to a workable democracy, but the fiction that political Parties could or would or should carry out the vast amount of pioneer thought and advance discussion which is essential in order to fill the gap between current politics, on the one hand, and industry, science and social services, on the other, is gradually being abandoned." [1]

Nor is it only the technical and scientific nature of modern politics which call for dispassionate and unprejudiced politicians. There is the moral need too. We shall certainly continue to need courage and self-sacrifice, and although in theory any Government ought to be bold enough, when necessary, to call for them, in practice only a National Government, which has been rid of all anxiety as to how opponents, committed to opposition, may exploit so exacting a demand, is likely to muster the necessary resolution. This may seem too derogatory a view of Governments, but I am afraid that it is fully justified by history, and in particular by the crisis of 1931, in which, whether or not the policy of reducing payments to the unemployed was wise, only a National Government had the courage to stand or fall by it, and was overwhelmingly justified by the event. Indeed even more recent history suggests, as we shall see, that not even

[1] *Ibid.*

a National Government is always bold enough to summon the whole nation to self-sacrifice.

Two other virtues in a National Government will make it indispensable. One is the comparative speed with which it can act; the Parliamentary machine being what it is, emergency procedure apart, only Ministers with a very powerful majority can pass a succession of important measures rapidly. And only friendly critics, not tempted to oppose for the sake of opposing, will long refrain from the temptation to oppose non-contentious legislation in order to delay subsequent contentious proposals. The other is what may be called its liberty of manœuvre. It is essential in war, and it will be essential after the war, that the Government should not be confined to the nostrums of the past; still less, of course, to those of any one Party. It must matter neither what Gladstone said in 1880, or Joseph Chamberlain in 1890, or Keir Hardie in 1900. The filial reverence of a Party for the programmes and the pronouncements of the past can be infinitely restrictive. In a phase of crisis it is essential that Ministers should be free to select their weapons from all the traditional armouries, or from none of them. And by the nature of its being, a National Government owes fewer hostages than any other to the past.

§ 8

Although discussion of the Party system led me to make some remarks on foreign policy, I set out in this chapter to consider some of the mechanics of democracy and not its beliefs, its political system and not its politics, still less their results. And there is one other main and integral feature of the political system as to which some of the experiences of war-time have prompted a fairly general outbreak of misgiving. One should not, after all, think of Parliament and Ministers without thinking of the Civil Service, which first obtains, and selects, the information on which Ministers found their plans, and then suggests, shapes, and finally executes their policy. Certain merits in the Civil Service are by now taken, and justifiably, for granted—which need not blind us to the fact that they are very solid, and on the whole very uncommon merits. Our bureaucracy is uncorrupt, industrious, conscientious, and, within wide limits, impartial. It contains a high proportion of the sort of ability which can be detected by written examinations. Writing, for an American public, in 1940, Mr. Albert Viton described it as "not only among the most honest in the world, but, what is far more important, among the most creative, most capable, and least enslaved to deadening routine." All the same, there are many complaints nowadays of its failure to adapt itself to the conditions of war, of its slowness, rigidity and lack of imagination. For all this there are doubtless certain reasons inherent in the structure of the service itself. Dominated by the praiseworthy tradition that similar cases must be dealt with according to the same standards, it is naturally inclined to treat precedent as paramount. Its members are very seldom either dismissed or rapidly promoted, and enterprise is not their outstanding characteristic. It is not an adventurous career, and the adventurous do not enter it; in peace-time half the candidates at College scholarship examinations at the Universities are aiming at the Civil Service, and three out of five will tell you that they do so because it is "safe." But the most disquieting charge against it—and I have heard it made recently by men of the widest experience, occupying positions in which they were in constant contact with many different Ministries—is that, on the whole, at a time when we need supremely competent administration, its members are no longer of adequate ability. This may be partly due to the increased competition of other careers. And there are plenty of critics who would explain, almost automatically, that what is wrong is that the Administrative Grade is recruited exclusively from the public schools. This, however, is not even true: it is recruited from the Universities, but by no means exclusively from the public schools: Mr. Chamberlain's adviser, Sir Horace Wilson, for example, was not a public school product: and France, in whose administration traditionalism and timidity were rampant as they never have been here, has never had a public school tradition. The fundamental reason for the defects of the Civil Service is one which was hinted at in the last chapter. It is recruited by literary examination. Any one who has taught the young men who obtain Firsts in the literary Schools at the Universities, and can therefore be tolerably certain of passing into the Administrative Grade, knows that a considerable proportion of them are never likely to possess much judgment or initiative. I remember meeting a gentleman holding a responsible Government post shortly before the evacuation from Dunkirk, who remarked that it did not really matter how far the German Army got; it did not matter if it got to London; for sooner or later it was bound to run out of oil, and then Germany would be finished—even if the German Army was in London. He had obtained three Firsts in his day, and had been a Professor in a famous University. Judgment in practical affairs is a rare quality which cannot be acquired from books, nor tested by literary examinations, while that well-marked class of examinees whose success depends upon the voracious absorption of other people's ideas are among the last persons in the world likely to display initiative. Nor, if he does not possess these qualities already, is the civil servant given much opportunity of acquiring them. Except in the Foreign and Colonial Offices, administrators spend their official careers without first-hand experience in the field. They continue to see life at second-hand, on paper. They are administrators who have never been administered, and too seldom make direct contact with the problems they handle. There is no advanced specialised training in the modern techniques of organisation and management, on the analogy of the Imperial Defence College. In the future radical changes will be needed in the selection and organisation of the service. When education is directed, as it ought to be, far more than ever before, to the co-ordinated training of mind, body and character, it may prove best to select civil servants on their academic records, and a searching personal interview. In their early years they should be brought into as much contact as possible with men and things outside the office, and the office files. And it will certainly be wise to see that failures are more frequently and more easily got rid of. Here, too, what we need is intellect and character in combination—exceptional intellect founded on sound character, or exceptional character combined with sound intellect. Here, too, we have been over-ready to look for intellect only, and to take other qualities for granted.

There is doubtless much that is wrong with democracy and its works; we should hardly find ourselves in our present plight if there were not. Nor does the fact that there is no doubt much more that is wrong with the despotisms dispense us from responsibility for our own shortcomings, though it may tempt us to forget them. With some of our failings, indeed, and with the prospect of purging ourselves of them in the fires, I shall do my best to deal in the next chapter. But as, I hope, this chapter has suggested, I do not think that those of them which go deepest are the direct consequence of our political machinery.

VI

PRODUCTION AND DISTRIBUTION—
FOR WHAT?

§ 1

Is it possible, in the lurid light of war, to see further
into the living structure of Britain than ever before, and
to see more clearly? Undoubtedly it is. Are there defects,
and virtues, in our social and economic organisation
apparent for the first time, or more fully apparent than
hitherto? Undoubtedly there are. But since this is the
vast scene which I wish to view, I must begin by saying
something of the personal standpoint from which I am
bound to view it.

I believe in the Christian doctrine of the Fall of man.
This doctrine asserts that man is now a creature full of
evil, and ill-adapted to the universe in which he lives, not
because God made him so, but because he was given free-
will, which necessarily includes the possibility of both
good and evil, and he misused it. This, it may be noted, is
a doctrine as to which science has nothing to say, either
for it or against. The form which the Fall, allegorically
represented in the book of Genesis by the story of the
apple of knowledge, may actually have assumed, is
vividly imagined, within the framework of both religion
and science, in what Mr. C. S. Lewis calls a myth, in the
Socratic sense of a revealing and not unlikely tale, in a
very remarkable chapter of his very remarkable book,
The Problem of Pain, which I respectfully commend to
any one interested in an extraordinarily lucid discussion
of the ultimate realities. But it is sufficient here to say
that, whatever the original Fall may have been, its

counterpart is constantly being re-enacted within our own experience, in the terrible choice between God and self made every day of each individual life, and by every civilisation in every age. We are "members of a spoiled species," and every age of mankind, like every day in the life of every individual, is in greater or less degree a Fall, a turning away from the true destiny of man, and from the true sources of his well-being. P   the age ushered in by the Industrial Revolution was in a special sense a Fall. The Industrial Revolution was to mean, of course, a steady succession of scientific discoveries and vast increases of material power, but it was to mean also, and for that very reason, that many ancient and indispensable truths would be gradually forgotten, and that moral and spiritual powers which men had exercised for centuries would be allowed to atrophy. By the end of the nineteenth century there were whole domains of human experience in which cultured Europeans were as ignorant as is a savage of electricity. And by the end of the nineteenth century much of Christendom was so sunk in self-will and gross appetite that it had become almost wholly blind to those eternal laws of individual and social well-being for neglect of which men and nations must sooner or later inevitably pay the price. Now from this vast spiritual regress there follow certain consequences which it is necessary to understand before we can hope to grasp either the meaning of our present troubles, or the prospects of escape from them.

In the first place, it is possible, and indeed easy, for an individual or a nation which has fallen into this degree of moral and spiritual sickness, to remain almost wholly, and almost always, unaware of its malady. To one living within the narrow limits of what Aristotle called the appetitive life, all may even seem to be well. We acquire

148

comfort, power or reputation, the world speaks well of us, we are conscious of being learned or intelligent or humane. And all the while there are divine laws to which we are as far from having surrendered our wills, and spiritual truths which we are as far from having comprehended as is a deaf man from being able to enjoy a Beethoven sonata—with this unhappy distinction, that the deaf man will probably at least be prepared to accept the assurance of musicians that a world of music, of which he knows nothing, does exist. And so in an age of spiritual apostasy and myopia it is possible for the leaders of the nation to display admirable records of humanitarian zeal, courageous statesmanship or devotion to science, and yet despite all to be irremediably *blind*. Such men will be wise and admirable persons, pursuing wise and admirable policies—*once you grant their moral assumptions, and their mental limitations*. Somewhere in *Anna Karenina* Tolstoy says, in effect, that philosophy makes sense, once you have accepted its jargon. A Christian spectator of modern life, with its assumption that the goal of society is a higher standard of living, will often be conscious of this same sense of a world which makes sense if he shares its assumptions, but makes sad nonsense if he does not. And what is more, since many of our rulers will not know that they are partially blind, since they are scarcely more conscious of the spiritual forces which rule the universe than a fly on the windscreen of an automobile of the principles of the internal-combustion engine, it is likely that they will assume that the best that can be hoped of the future is that in it they should contrive to do more successfully what they have tried to do in the past. They will look forward to little more than a good time being had by all, at the same moral level at which they have attempted to provide a good time for all hitherto. The goal of man will continue to be a higher standard of living. They will not be able to imagine, and in all good faith they will ridicule any one who suggests to them, the possibility that to found civilisation on the appetites of atheism can never, in the long run, lead to anything but disaster. Sir Alfred Zimmern [1] tells of a conversation between von Hügel and a religiously minded and "progressive" employer who was proposing, as he supposed, to "christianise" his factory by the introduction of every sort of comfort and welfare organisation for his work-people. Von Hügel broke in angrily upon his description of these material blessings: "You haven't begun to understand what Christianity is. Christianity is not refreshment bars and swimming pools—it is a soul in the presence of God." And this fashionable illusion will be reinforced by another, less obvious, which survives from the last century. In that hey-day of fast-developing material resources, in which the latest theory seemed as surely an advance as the latest machine, all history was thought of as a struggle between "progress" and the forces of resistance. In fact, as we can see easily enough now, neither party in this imaginary conflict could ever have defined its aims. Progress towards what? For most contemporaries the standard was merely quantitative; progress was to prolong the line AB. Income-tax is sixpence in the pound. Then income-tax at a shilling in the pound is progress. If wages or profits have risen, it is progress that they should rise still further.

"After a change has been initiated—the extension of the franchise, the raising of income-tax, the shortening of the hours of work, the provision of social services

[1] *Spiritual Values and World Affairs*, 23.

by the state—all that one has to do is to decide the pace. Any one can initiate a new departure, and as long as it does not obviously oppose existing movements, it is 'progress.' [1]

This characteristic assumption, that the goal of progress, which is to-day the object of human life, does not need to be defined, is very marked in most of the numerous books and brochures, published by individuals, Parties and semi-official organisations during the last decade, on the Planning of the future. The drabness which many readers will have noted in them is largely due to the fact that they simply ignore both value and purpose. To compare a modern work on Planning with, say, Plato's Republic (which is also a work on Planning) is a striking lesson in the difference between a civilisation which concerns itself with Ends and a civilisation which is conscious only of Means.

And, if it comes to that, resistance to what? Those who resisted change, too, seldom knew of any principle on which to select the changes which they were to resist. A half-hearted attempt to slow down all change, and an unquestioning acceptance of their opponents' misty opinions as to what progress was, this was usually the best that they could manage. In so far as this twofold illusion survives to-day, of mere quantitative advance in a direction already determined, it can but reinforce the blind impulse to revive and extend, as soon as circumstances permit, the sort of good time for all at which most politicians have aimed in the past. There have been exceptions, of course, to this crude, but roughly accurate, generalisation as to the illusion which made all Parties in the state assume the inevitability of an un-

---

[1] Michael Roberts, *The Recovery of the West*, 80-1.

reflecting, quantitative "progress" towards undefined goals. The young Disraeli's criticism of Peel's Tamworth Manifesto of 1834 as "an attempt to found a Party without principles" shewed that he was at least aware of the ineptitude of a Conservatism which did not know what it was to conserve, while the romantic creed of the Young England group of the early 'forties, in which he was the moving spirit, did contrive, somewhat obscurely, to suggest the principle of what we should now call function, as a test for the fitness of an institution to survive. Similarly it may be said that the school of Bentham and Mill, of which Gladstone eventually became the political protagonist, would have defined progress as the growth of rationalism or, perhaps more confidently, of humanitarianism. This, however, does not take us much further. In the last analysis rationalism was no more than the deification of that very blindness which made so much of the nineteenth century squalid, and so much of the twentieth disastrous. While, though humanitarianism is certainly a virtue, it is a virtue which it is dangerously easy to attribute to ourselves—"I can't bear cruelty," we say, though we have never made the least sacrifice for a fellow-creature—nor does it by any means necessarily follow that the growth of humanitarianism is a sufficient compensation for the simultaneous decay of other qualities. Different ages cultivate different virtues, and each is tempted to suppose that the virtue which it happens to profess excuses it for the lack of all those which it ignores.

"If, then, you are ever tempted to think that we modern Western Europeans cannot really be so very bad, because we are, comparatively speaking, humane —if, in other words, you think God might be content with us on that ground—ask yourself whether you think God ought to have been content with the cruelty of cruel ages because they excelled in courage or chastity. You will see at once that this is an impossibility. From considering how the cruelty of our ancestors looks to us, you may get some inkling how our softness, worldliness, and timidity would have looked to them, and hence how both must look to God." [1]

The first conclusion from the special version of the Fall which has been enacted during the last hundred years is negative. We may, I think, be sure that this war is not being fought in order that we may continue to concern ourselves solely with Means, or resume, upon a more lavish scale, the interminable quest for a materialist's "good time." It is an exposure, not a justification, of the illusion that "progress" is a higher standard of living.

§ 2

But there is a further conclusion to be drawn, and it is positive, suggesting what the present war does mean, rather than what it does not. It is to be found in the nature of pain. Most pain, perhaps, is the mere consequence of the wickedness or folly of mankind, and is therefore, in a sense, purposeless. Granted free-will, men will torture each other; granted free-will, there will be folly and sin, and it is in the nature of folly and sin that their consequences should fall often upon the innocent. But much pain is also purposeful and remedial. The Fall which is constantly being re-enacted in human history is,

[1] C. S. Lewis, *The Problem of Pain*, 63.

in essence, a refusal to surrender self to the divine laws of the universe, and recovery, the rendering back of the will long claimed for self, is bound to be painful. It is indeed a kind of death, a "mortification" of the self. Moreover, just as physical pain is often the finger-post which points to disease, mental pain is often the unmasking of sin and error. Until the sinner is brought up short by pain, he has no notion that his way of life does not "answer" to the laws of the universe. If he is to be redeemed, "the creature's illusion of self-sufficiency must be shattered." And it is within the experience of most of us that the unexpected threat of mortal disease, or the sudden prospect that the world we know is about to collapse about our ears, will shake us, for the moment, out of our customary self-sufficiency, and startle us into a sense of our dependence upon something beyond and above the world with which we are customarily content. Mr. C. S. Lewis observes that these familiar human experiences imply a strange degree of what he calls Divine humility: for it is a poor thing to turn back to the eternal, only because the ship is going down under us, and there is nothing now better to be had, to surrender our self-centred lives only when they are no longer worth keeping. "It is hardly complimentary to God that we should choose Him as an alternative to Hell, yet even this He accepts."

Nor of course are these remedial experiences confined to the life of the individual. The writings of the Old Testament prophets are very largely the record of a people which turned to God in adversity, and forgot Him when it waxed prosperous. The Indian poet, Rabindranath Tagore, has recorded his impressions of the Germany of 1921, whose spirit was still seared and purged by adversity.

" Germany to-day has received a violent check on her political ambitions. This has produced an almost universal longing in her midst to seek for spiritual resources within, in place of external success. Germany appears now to have set out on a voyage of spiritual adventure. And in spite of her dire poverty, she is not thinking merely of . . . some new move in the political game of gambling, but rather of the achievement of that inner freedom, which gives us power to soar above the vicissitudes of circumstances." [1]

And he goes on:

" The other day, I met the British Ambassador in Berlin. While alluding to the enormous appreciation of my works in Germany, he expressed his feeling of gratification at the possibility of my supplying some philosophy which might bring consolation to these people. He was glad, I am sure, from his British point of view. He seemed to me to imagine that philosophy was a soothing draught, which might lull the restless activity of the German nation into sleep, affording the victors a better security in their enjoyment of material benefits. He would gladly concede the possession of Soul and God to these people, only keeping for the share of his own nation, the possession of the worldly goods. He seemed to smile, as it were, in his sleeve and to imagine that his own British people would be the gainers in the bargain." [1]

We know now how soon, if it ever indeed set out, the German "voyage of spiritual adventure" was shipwrecked. But we cannot shut our eyes to the truth that, if only

[1] Rabindranath Tagore, *Letters from Abroad*, 137, 138.

adversity will turn us from the things which are not to the things which are, then adversity may be what we need. Very briefly and very crudely stated, these are some of the reasons why pain is remedial, and why regeneration must be painful. During the last hundred years, the hey-day of materialism, we have in a special sense been blind followers of the blind. Our recovery could hardly have been painless, even if it had come about of our own volition: for "to surrender a self-will inflamed and swollen with years of usurpation is a kind of death." But it has not come about of our own volition. If we do recover, and it is not yet certain that we shall, it will be because we have passed through the fires of war. Pain will have performed its ancient, remedial function, un-masking for us our sins and errors, and shattering our illusion of self-sufficiency. We shall have achieved re-generation through suffering. No one, surely, who can believe at all in the presence of design in human destiny, can doubt that this is the design of the war. And if this is the design, or one design, of the war, to offer us a last chance of regeneration, then we must indeed hope that the world after the war will be a different place to the world we have so far known; qualitatively, not only quantitatively, different, a New Order indeed.

But nobody who believes that man has Fallen, that by nature, and failing a deliberate and painful effort of his own, he is spiritually maladjusted to the Universe, can suppose that, however wise and fortunate we may prove, we are likely to produce the New Jerusalem on earth of which politicians are so apt to talk. This is the illusion of the Radical, who believes that one root and branch reform of the political or social system can cure every ill. It is the illusion indeed of all the Utopians who believe that some alteration or other in our communal arrangements will produce a permanently happy and prosperous society. Such men forget that society is only a large number of individuals, and that, whatever the political or economic system, imperfect individuals are bound to mean an imperfect society. In so far as its citizens are greedy and faithless, the state will be disfigured by faithlessness and greed. This sounds a simple observation enough, and it is surprising that it should be so regularly overlooked. It follows from it that there can be no lasting or extensive reform of the state without reform of the individuals of whom the state is composed, and that the fashionable blueprints of New Social Orders which have no word to say of new individual standards are largely waste-paper. This is not comfortable doctrine, for it is much easier to discuss the reform of Britain or Europe or the world, for all of which our personal responsibility is extremely small, than the reform of ourselves, for which no one but ourselves is responsible at all, and which we are likely to find extremely painful. Nevertheless it is a truth, which we can forget if we please, but cannot escape.

§ 3

So much for the personal standpoint from which I am bound to view the present scene. And now let us see how our special failings during the last hundred years have issued in the problems of social and economic organisation by which we are chiefly perplexed in wartime. I have already referred to one familiar intellectual consequence of nineteenth-century material progress, the illusion which it fostered that, because the latest machine almost inevitably outmoded the last but one, therefore the latest philosophy, cult or fashion was equally certain to represent an advance upon its predecessors. Since Samuel Smiles lived nearly two thousand years after Plato, he was nearly two thousand years more up to date. The other familiar distemper bred by material progress was the excessive importance which men came to set upon comfort, and the excessive respect which they paid to wealth. Here again we were partly saved by the instinct for compromise. We have never acknowledged, as the United States has come near to acknowledging, a mere hierarchy of riches; we have had no "grading lists" of millionaires in Britain, for here there have always been several conflicting social standards, and several separate hierarchies, each helping to keep the others in their place. There has been an aristocracy of birth—somebody has said that the chief merit of the aristocrat is to laugh at the plutocrat, and the prime function of the plutocrat to laugh at the aristocrat—which has encouraged some people to admire ancestry instead of riches. And there has been another aristocracy, emphasised by the award of public honours for distinguished achievement, which has done a great deal to maintain the old tradition that public service is preferable to private acquisition. Even so, during the last hundred years mere riches have probably been more generally respected than at any other period in our history—partly no doubt because many rich men were more respectable, and partly because they were more powerful, than hitherto; but to a considerable extent because wealth and comfort were held to be more enviable than ever before. The grasping Victorian capitalist, and the hideous trail of slums which acquisitive Victorian capitalism spread across the country, are a familiar tale. It was our misfortune that the coming of the machine had coincided with the zenith of the doctrine of laisser-faire (though it is not difficult to trace a causal connection between the two), and, since this was the prototype of industrial revolutions, it was for us to make the first mistakes, some of which, observing our painful example, other countries were subsequently able to avoid. Nevertheless greed and materialism lay at the roots of the Victorian system, and have infected almost everything which grew in that soil ever since. Even the idealists of the Victorian era could be idealists in terms of the drabbest materialism. "You may reason," wrote Cobden, "ever so logically, but never so convincingly as through the pocket. But it will take time . . . John Bull . . . will not be easily persuaded that all his reliance upon brute force and courage has been a losing speculation." [1] Dean Inge has suggested that:

"Socialism and Communism belong to the same circle of ideas as acquisitive Capitalism. Both regard the possession of money and the things which money can buy as the supreme good. Both are out of date as soon as a different standard is accepted" [2]

Of the creeds of some Socialists this is no doubt grotesquely untrue. There have been plenty of unworldly Socialists, such as Bruce Glasier, who dreamed of a society inspired by the spirit of service, and artist Socialists like William Morris, who dreamed of a world which once more believed in beauty. Nevertheless of a very large number of Socialists, and particularly of "class-conscious" Socialists, Dean Inge's words are painfully true. For these Socialists Socialism is little more than a means of

[1] Letter to John Bright, Dec. 23, 1848. Morley, *Life of Cobden*, 503.
[2] *The Fall of the Idols*, 153.

enriching themselves at the expense of somebody else, and in the world of political morality they are on the same low level as the Conservatives for whom Conservatism is merely a means of preventing somebody else from acquiring their property. I remember a rich Conservative Member of Parliament saying with passionate conviction, "If you lay hands on my property, I shall draw my revolver." I know of owner-skippers of small trawlers who make a net income of from £30 to £70 a week, who have never paid a penny of income-tax, and are quite incapable of seeing why they should pay income-tax, but profess an ardent Socialism, on the ground that Socialism intends to tax to extinction the riches of the wealthy. The two conceptions of politics are identical. Similarly a grasping materialism could not be expected long to remain the exclusive prerogative of the employer. The Trade Unionism which grew up after 1850 has had many merits—with the Public School it has been one of the two great formative influences of our time—but in large degree it has been founded on the acceptance of the principles which were practised by the employer. In the world of labour these are doubtless to a large extent discounted by the simplicity of their environment, and the fraternal element and Friendly Society activities in the unions were of real moral value. Nor is a poor man endeavouring to become less poor in quite the same ethical category as a rich man trying to protect his riches. Nevertheless, in such a society too many of the unions were bound, like too many of the employers, to concern themselves more with their own reward than with their service to the state. They, too, accepted the materialist dogma of the capitalist, that the end of life is the standard of living. Between 1888 and 1918 the wage-cost of coal-getting rose by 280 per cent, while, in spite of many

160

mechanical advances, the output per person employed
fell from 299 tons to 224 tons per annum. And the contagion of the materialist appetites which had so deeply
penetrated the economic organisation turned much
Socialism sour, at times degrading a creed which, in
origin and theory, is benevolently concerned with the
welfare of all society, into something like a venomous
declaration of civil war. " It is the great value of the
General Strike that it overturns Society absolutely."
"Although it is not as a rule wise to offer physical violence
to blacklegs, there is nothing wrong about it except in
the eyes of the law and the middle classes" (Mr. G. D. H.
Cole). "In the class war all weapons are justifiable" (Mr.
W. Mellor).

These sentences, written by men of distinction and pro-
bity in the most bitter and appetitive phase of Socialism
a decade or so ago, would hardly have been recognised
as his spiritual progeny by Sir Thomas More, of the
Utopia, the first English Socialist, and they almost
deserve the comment of Dean Inge, who quotes them.[1]

It was natural that comfort should become the ideal
of such an age as this, and there were very many who
would probably have been ready to define progress itself
as consisting of more humanitarianism and more comfort. Thus Mr. Sinclair Lewis has explained that one
of the reasons why he could not believe in the divinity
of Christ, was that in an age of squalor and disease He
omitted to reveal to His contemporaries the fundamental
principles of sanitation; and this notion—that the Christian revelation cannot be divine since it omitted to ex-
pound the mysteries of modern American plumbing—
is entirely "period". A slowly spreading softness, the
hatred of hardship, danger and sacrifice, is perhaps in-

[1] *The Fall of the Idols.*

evitably the obverse of the cult of kindness and the pursuit of comfort. Indeed reluctance to face sacrifices, save under the spur of extreme danger, is the weakness most natural to a democracy, conspicuous enough in the record of Britain, and even more obvious in that of the United States, during the last twenty years. Indeed it may be that there is a causal connection between naval power, democracy and the disinclination for living strenuously in peace-time. The most powerful navy makes comparatively insignificant demands upon man-power, and is virtually invisible to the mass of the people. Unlike a powerful army, it neither subjects a nation to the rigours of discipline nor serves as a constant reminder of them. It confers the maximum of power with the minimum of conscious sacrifice. The weaknesses latent in the free, inquiring genius of naval Athens did not become apparent until, in the Peloponnesian war, she faced the military people of Lacedaemon, infinitely her inferior in everything except their lifelong habit of discipline and sacrifice; the Romans, a nation of soldiers which possessed no navy at the commencement of the Punic war, eventually outfought the empire of Carthage, founded upon sea-power, thanks to the tough fibre of a people bred to hardship and danger.

When we remember the principal elements in the mental climate of the last hundred years—the love of freedom, with its obverse, the distaste for discipline; the cult of humanitarianism, with its obverse, the inclination to softness; the pursuit of comfort and wealth; the widespread agnosticism as to the purpose of human existence—the economic structure of British society, paradoxical enough at first sight, begins to appear intelligible and natural. We realise the inevitability of an organisation of industry sufficiently collectivist to meet the demand for state regulation and large-scale enterprise, yet not collectivist enough to encroach seriously upon the liberty of the individual. The attempt to make the best of both worlds becomes intelligible when we remember that state control can be both the necessary remedy for economic abuses and the necessary source of industrial efficiency, and also at the same time the formidable instrument of personal servitude. We see, too, how natural is the corollary, a system of social insurance whose merit is that it protects the weak, and whose defect that it encourages a majority of citizens to think of the state as something from which they expect benefits rather than something to which they owe duties, so that we understand how symptomatic is the tone in which, for example, a recent issue of *Time and Tide* estimates the social achievement of the last few decades, applauding ". . . an improved pattern of life in which a greater number of benefits are made available to a greater number of people. The national share-out may not yet have gone a long way but it has at least begun." We can understand how a nominally Christian country has come to exclude Christianity from an integral rôle in its national life. And this not only thanks to the materialism natural to the age of the machine; for the social services and the factories together unite to undermine that sharp sense of personal responsibility which is essential to religious faith. The social services remove from the individual many obligations and many decisions which are proper to family life. And the factories breed a mechanical lack of initiative in those who tend the machines: so that, as those who know them well will agree, there is much less individuality and enterprise among factory workers than among miners or railwaymen.

§ 4

We fashion our own destiny. These weaknesses, the legacy of an age whose chief defect it was to have become too greedy, too soft and too unbelieving, take shape to-day as precisely those problems which most notably beset us in time of war, and which we have therefore to show ourselves capable of solving, if we are to deserve to survive, and to shape another age. They can be summed up, perhaps, in three questions, which are now being asked day in and day out by men and women of every type and class. Firstly, can a system which is part collectivist, part individualist generate the greatest possible efficiency—now that to generate the greatest possible efficiency is a matter of life and death? We are doing our best to have the best of both worlds; may we in fact be ensuring for ourselves the worst? Is there too much state interference, or too little? Sometimes we find ourselves making the one complaint, sometimes the other. Sometimes we ask, why will not the Government give us more orders, and less advice? Why did it advise farmers in the summer of 1940 to build their ricks in the centre of their fields, and parents to evacuate their children from the industrial centres, or have them inoculated against typhoid? Why did it invite householders with iron railings to hand them over for scrap iron, and owners of field-glasses to give, or sell, them for the armed forces? Why did it not compel all these citizens to do these things? Why did the Home Secretary make no serious arrangements for fire-fighting until after a large part of the City of London had been burned to the ground, and why did he even then for a long while not make fire-fighting compulsory? Why, in short, have so much skill and energy been allowed to go untapped, so many unnecessary inequalities been bred, simply because there have been no orders? At least as often, however, as we criticise the reluctance of the Government to govern, we find ourselves complaining of its irritating, or ineffective, intrusions on our private lives. Farmers and small agricultural producers are exasperated by the snow-storm of unintelligible Forms which they are repeatedly having to fill up; or the rector of a parish in an "enclosed area," absent on war service, cannot return home for a few days' leave without permission from the billeting-officer; and people are tempted to ask whether we have forgotten that we are fighting to preserve liberty. Or the Government steps in to control the distribution of eggs, and immediately we hear of villages, hitherto plentifully supplied from their own doorsteps, whose own eggs are laboriously transported to remote destinations and replaced by an irregular and inadequate trickle laboriously imported from equally remote sources; and we exclaim that government interference always means confusion and delay.

§ 5

The second of the three questions, now so often asked, which may be said to sum up the war-time perplexities which we inherit from our pre-war failings, concerns the Government's reluctance to impose full economic sacrifice upon either the powerful or the many. Would not the reasonable and courageous course, we ask, have been to have imposed an Excess Profits Duty on *everybody* at the outbreak of war? Why should anybody, save those already on the genuine poverty line, be better off because the nation is fighting for its life? Why should so much

profiteering be permitted, at both ends of the economic
scale? What, at one end, of the contractor working
on cost plus profit who deliberately slows down work
on some vital piece of production because it pays
him for it to last longer? Again, whatever the nominal
level of the actual Excess Profits Duty, who doubts that
there are plenty of methods of camouflaging profits,
and that many owners, manufacturers, and merchants
are in fact making a very good thing out of the war?
But, partly no doubt because excessive profits have long
been so familiar a feature of the social landscape, and
partly because what excessive profits there are now are
necessarily well camouflaged, it is not upon the war
profiteering of the few, but upon excessive wages, the
war-profiteering of the many, that (not altogether
logically) public interest usually fastens as symptomatic
of the Government's reluctance to impose sacrifices on
those who are in a position to resist them. Why, we ask,
should the wife of a serving soldier pinch on a separation
allowance of twenty-five shillings a week, while the wife
of his neighbour, a munitions worker, can buy fur coats
on fifteen pounds a week? Is it not as unreasonable, we
ask, for a factory worker in war-time to be able to throw
up work on vital production for another job which
happens to be better paid—as if a private in a Tank
regiment were in a position to inform his colonel that he
proposed to leave his unit next Monday, because he has
been offered higher wages in the Army Pay Corps? Why
do not the factories imitate here the thoroughgoing
Socialism of the Army? In the first twenty-one months
of the war, wages rose by four million pounds a week,
and most of these increases were frankly demanded on the
ground that taxes and prices were going up—with the
implication that, although the community as a whole

obviously could not win the war without paying for it, this powerful section was to remain sheltered from all economic sacrifice. The economist, naturally enough, is chiefly impressed by the destructive inflationary effect of unrestricted wage-increases—the vicious spiral, as he ca¹¹ it, which may eventually ruin us all, higher prices stimulating higher wages, and higher wages, in their turn, higher prices—but it is with the moral, not the economic consequences, that we are now concerned. And the moral interrogation-marks involved are formidable. Every one, presumably, would agree that the earnings of all who before the war were on the borderline of hardship ought to rise, in advance, even, of rising costs. But as to the vast majority, above that borderline? Can we expect to earn victory, and survival, without reaching the moral level at which the whole community will accept economic sacrifice? Mr. Michael Roberts has observed, in *The Recovery of the West*, that Socialism fails where it becomes necessary to demand sacrifices, not from a privileged minority, but from the people themselves. But may not this be the crucial moral test, not of Socialism only, but of democracy? Are we suffering from the taint of commercialism, spread now to both ends of the income-scale? Socialism has done well to denounce high profits in peace-time; has it done well to refrain from denouncing high wages in war-time? Is not the moral principle the same—no private advantage out of the nation's peril, the principle, in fact, of service, the principle of Socialism, the principle of the Navy, the Army and the Air Force? More pay for more work, but not more pay for the same work, because we are at war? We are measuring our strength with the system of compulsion, under which the whole nation is forced to accept deliberately imposed economic hardship, whether it likes it or not; can we hope to wriggle through the testing-time without making an altogether equivalent sacrifice ourselves? May not Mr. Bevin's declaration that he likes to see wages rise, though natural enough from a trade union leader, be an anachronism, and a dangerous one, in a member of the War Cabinet? Such are the long-term implications of the reluctance to face sacrifice, complete and comprehensive. As to what may be called the short-term implications, the effects on our immediate war-effort, the evidence is contradictory, but in some ways disquieting. Briefly, it may be said that the Fifteenth Report of the Government Committee on Expenditure declared that exceptionally high wages are responsible for a certain amount of absenteeism and slackness, and that Mr. Bevin says they are not. Some Members of Parliament have maintained that not more than one per cent of war workers are doing less than their best, others that laziness is dangerously widespread. One Member said that he knew of foremen drawing eighteen pounds a week in a local factory, who spent their time encouraging men to go slow, in order that the work might run on into overtime; others have claimed that nothing but occasional bad health and insufficient transport stands between British factories and the greatest output possible. The truth is probably somewhere between the two extreme views. All the same, it is rare indeed to listen to anybody with any sort of first-hand experience unburdening himself in private upon these matters, without hearing story after story which suggests that, thanks to the Government's reluctance to impose economic sacrifice on the many, the taint of commercialism, once presumed to be confined to the powerful, is spreading among the rank and file. Two tales which happen to have come my way of late suggest a pattern in these perplexing phenomena. A "productive war-worker" threw up his job in disgust because (he said) "there are only two men in that factory genuinely working. All they think about there is wages. If a man hasn't made ten pounds at the end of the week he often raffles whatever he has earned, and makes ten pounds out of the sale of tickets." A staff-officer in the Royal Air Force said: "A little while back my wife and I stayed for a few days in a country pub, where we shared our meals with a couple of craftsmen from a great aircraft factory nearby. I was astonished to find that they were only working three or four days a week, and apparently choosing whether they went to work or not according to mere personal whim. They told us that at the Government's request their factory had worked last Christmas and Boxing-day, on overtime pay of course, and then shut down for three days' clear holiday. I used to drive from that inn to my office, past about three hundred men putting down a new tarmac runway (which we needed mighty quickly), and I'll swear I never once saw a dozen of them working at the same time; in fact, to judge by what I did see, I'd guarantee to get as much work out of three boys as any dozen of those chaps. They were paid by the hour, of course, with overtime, and their boss got his costs plus ten per cent, so that the longer the job took the better, as far as he was concerned. Then, in the R.A.F., I'd find myself dealing with men who were tumbling over each other to take on the most dangerous jobs in the service—and often enough they were men who'd been ruined by the war, one-man businesses and so on—and were only drawing a pound or two a week in the Air Force." The contrast there is vivid enough, but it is a contrast, of course, between systems, not individuals. The aircraftmen who clamoured for a chance to risk their lives for a few shillings a week, as air-gunners or observers, were the sons or brothers of the men who raffled their wages or worked at half speed with an eye on overtime. But the airmen were members of a service which called on them for courage and self-sacrifice, while the craftsmen were in an over-commercialised industry where tradition and example alike encouraged them to think first of hard cash and their own advantage. We are creatures of our environment, and nine human beings out of ten will respond to the nature of the call made on them. It can be as simple as that.

§ 6

The third of the three questions which sum up our main war-time perplexities, and are now so often asked, is one which I have already had occasion to put myself, earlier in this book. An Oxford undergraduate who, after considerable hesitation, volunteered for the Navy early in the war, and is now an Ordinary Seaman, wrote to me of his early misgivings. "All the talk about fighting to defend Christianity simply sickened me. I know the public schools and Oxford, and bits of the East End of London pretty well, and I was brought up in the Home Counties, and I am pretty clear that this is a heathen country. I was doubtful about killing anyway, and the idea of killing on behalf of such hypocrisy as that was too much for me at first." It is the old question, the question I have already asked, and, in part, already tried to answer: Since in this war it is so clearly Christendom which is at stake, how can Britain hope for victory until it is a Christian country?

§7

I take this last of the three current questions first, for it is the fundamental one. We must not hope for victory, unless we have deserved it. And we shall not deserve it, unless we become actually the better for fighting, braced and buffeted into our truer selves. If this war does not mean moral and spiritual regeneration, it means moral and spiritual catastrophe. This time there is no middle way possible. But there cannot be moral and spiritual regeneration, unless, each in his own way, a vast majority of individual citizens contribute to the moral and spiritual effort of the nation, just as there cannot be military victory unless, each in his own way, a vast majority of individual citizens contribute to the military effort of the nation. Thus to shed one's own besetting self-indulgence is itself a contribution to the victory which has to be earned. But it is not likely that a majority of us will make the necessary moral contribution, unless a majority of us are Christians. And in any case, for a Christian, the need of moral and spiritual regeneration, which so many have begun to perceive, can only mean the need of becoming more Christian.

This applies equally, of course, to the new age after the war. Planners and New-social-orderers waste their pains when they lay out their New Jerusalems without any reference to the spiritual and moral condition of those who are to live in them. There can never be a New Jerusalem until its prospective inhabitants are fit to live in a New Jerusalem. The materialist, with his simple outlook and his quantitative standards, may suppose that progress can be measured; more houses, more cars, more wireless-sets, higher incomes; and that "more" education, a school-leaving age of fifteen instead of fourteen, of sixteen instead of fifteen, of seventeen instead of sixteen, is inevitably progress—characteristically overlooking the possibility that if the education is bad education, more of it will be not progress, but poison. There can be no settled happiness without moral well-being, and it can hardly be too often repeated that, since a nation consists of a great number of individuals, however numerous its wireless sets, however admirable its drainage, there can be no settled happiness for the nation, no New Jerusalem, in fact, unless a majority of the individuals who compose the nation have themselves achieved moral well-being. It is tempting enough to persuade oneself that laws alone can make a New Jerusalem, and that we can accordingly spare ourselves the painful process of self-reform, and this indeed may be why some of the most ardent public reformers have led notably disorganised and self-indulgent private lives. But without reform of ourselves we can no more expect effective reform of the state than we can hope for a powerful war-effort by the nation unless the individual contributes to it. Prohibition failed in the United States because it was a reform of the law not founded upon a reform of the citizen. The two processes, it is true, continually interact upon each other; some public reforms, the abolition of slavery or of slums, for example, will greatly raise the standard of personal morality. There have been times when no advance in individual standards could be expected until some public reform had been effected. Nevertheless in general the reform of ourselves is infinitely more important than the reform of the state, and it is certain that what democracy needs just now is not better organisation but better democracy. It is conceivable that a nation might live in misery under a political and economic system which was theoretically perfect, simply because its citizens were greedy, licentious and faithless, whereas if every citizen lived a Christian life almost any political and economic system would function admirably. No state can reach a moral level higher than that prevailing among its citizens. It follows that the most valuable public reforms are not those which give men more comfort or more wealth, but those which make it possible for them to become completer and more moral human beings. The success of the former, of course, is much easier to measure; the researches embodied in Mr. Seebohm Rowntree's *Poverty and Progress*, his conclusion that, while in 1899 15.46 per cent of the wage-earning population lived below his "poverty line" there were only 6.8 below the equivalent line in 1936, naturally give us a comfortable sensation of solid achievement. Indeed, to have made a great many poor people a good deal less poor is undoubtedly a solid achievement, but though it is probable that this decline in urban poverty has also been an advance in urban happiness, it is extremely difficult to prove it. Often enough reforms which make people better off, as we say, will also make them better, but they would be more likely to do so if more reformers thought it important that people should be better, and not merely better off.

Regeneration is indispensable if we are to earn victory, so runs the argument, and regeneration means, first and foremost, the regeneration of human beings of flesh and blood, painful though that process must inevitably be, and not the regeneration on paper of a bloodless abstraction called the state. For a Christian, regeneration must mean becoming more Christian. And therefore his answer to the question, how can a country which is not Christian expect to win a war in defence of Christendom? will be that it ought to expect no such thing, and that every step, every effort, towards a revival of Christian faith or practice should be actively encouraged, and treated as the necessary earnest, in war-time, of a much wider development after it. There is of course evidence of a revival of Christianity—I say "of course," for war always jolts men's minds beyond the immediate present, so that the religious turn to God, the materialists to the future, and the superstitious to the astrologers. But the sort of revival which will satisfy the Christian that his country is indeed earning its survival is one which appears to be striking roots wide and deep in the national life. In public affairs he will have three main concerns. For any one who has grasped the paramount importance of individual well-being, as the *sine qua non* of public well-being, education will naturally come first and foremost. Politicians clamouring for more education, whatever its quality, will appear as futile as a doctor prescribing more medicine, regardless of its ingredients. The time has come for us to make up our minds whether this is to be a Christian state, or not, for we cannot perpetually have it both ways, or continue indefinitely to claim the privileges and the prestige of a Christian community, without assuming its obligations. And if it is to be a Christian state, then its education must be Christian education. And Christian education means, at the least, that a substantial proportion of the teachers, of all subjects, should be Christians. A hundred years ago this would not have seemed a particularly lofty ideal, but to-day it is a formidable objective indeed. Formidable, in the first place, because, with the abolition of religious tests so fresh in the memory as one of the greatest triumphs of democracy, it will have to be a question of voluntary adjustment and compromise, and not of legislation. As to which all that need be said, perhaps, is that everything depends upon the "mental climate." A nation which genuinely wants Christian education will undoubtedly contrive to get it. A more formidable obstacle is the mental climate itself. That a large number of citizens eagerly desire a Christian revival in education is certain, and I believe myself that the nation as a whole would welcome it. The obstacles to be surmounted are rather the contemptuous opposition of a small number of influential materialists and agnostics, for whose opinions the general public has long been trained to feel a quite unnecessary deference, reinforced by the natural timidity of bureaucrats and politicians. In the elementary schools some religious instruction for all, except those whose parents do not wish them to have it; and instruction by competent teachers; that is what the Archbishops' demand, of February, 1941, amounted to. It is a modest demand, much more modest than that suggested above, but when, in the following August, a deputation representing the Anglican and Free Churches put it before the President of the Board of Education, an exceptionally able and respected Minister, but, like most Presidents of the Board of Education, very recently appointed, his reply was plentifully studded with phrases at least as familiar as the sympathy, traditionally professed by almost all Ministers to almost all deputations, and, it is to be feared, a good deal more significant. "The deputation would appreciate that, before giving formal answers . . . he would need . . . detailed consultation;" "he would . . . explore;" "without further consideration, he would hesitate to interfere with it;" "the matter was one for consultation with the other interests concerned;" "it did not appear to him to be easy . . . but he would consider the proposal;" "he would hesitate, without further consideration, to interfere with the domesticities of the schools;" "he was sure that they, on their side, would understand the necessity of a full and sympathetic examination of the questions at issue." Such are some of the ringing and decisive phrases with which the President of the Board of Education received the request of the Churches for competent religious instruction in the schools of a professedly Christian state, engaged in a life-and-death struggle to preserve Christendom.[1] It will not be easy to revive Christian education in the state schools, and there, almost as much as in the secondary and public schools, it is likely to be a question of voluntary adjustment rather than legislation. A formidable task, certainly, but not an impossible one.

An equally serious concern of those who see that their country must earn its survival, and believe that a Christian revival is necessary to its doing so, will be the home. The family has always been the basis of the Christian social system, and there can be no other. The Christian statesman will always tend to think of humanity not in terms of the state, nor even of the individual, but of the family. As a serving soldier has written recently, claiming to speak for countless ordinary men:

"The centre of any good world is our own home and our own family. The test of any political system, of any religious philosophy, is its effect upon the homes of the people, and . . . upon family life."[2]

All the greatest social advances, from Habeas Corpus to slum clearance, have been made in defence of the home.

---

[1] All who know the present Minister will recognise that this is evidence, not of his own indifference but of the 'mental climate' of the Day, in which he has to work.

[2] *A Soldier's New World* by Sappers D. H. Barber and M. Hollmes, 2.

It is the home which determines the moral level of the state, and it does not matter very much what education is provided in the classroom, if its effects are obliterated in the home. In recent years, however, there have been formidable attacks, both material and moral, upon home and family. The industrial revolution, and the appearance of the urban slum, destroyed or polluted family life for very many. Even to-day the evidence of the war-time evacuations reminds us that home-life in the industrial areas must often be startlingly unworthy of the citizens of a great Commonwealth. For some while moreover, and particularly during the last two decades, the very ideas of the home and the family have had to face a powerful offensive from the propagandists of moral disintegration. Influential voices have commended sexual licence, and urged the loosening of family ties. "It is possible . . .", wrote one modern student of marriage,

"to visualise a future in which the State will have assumed practically all the functions of parenthood, in which the children will not necessarily live at home, and in which the association of the actual parents with their children will be limited to those periods of leisure when both parents and children are free from their normal occupation . . ." [1]

Fortunately, ordinary humanity has always hotly resented and stoutly resisted this tendency to substitute the bureaucrat for the parent, which is endemic among those who see men and women as mere Planner's fodder, the bloodless material of graphs and statistics. The author of *A Soldier's New World* claims to be speaking for the average man, when he writes:

[1] Ralph de Pomeroi, *Marriage, Past, Present and Future*, 321.

"The ordinary man demands the *means* to give his son a long education, but he claims the right to decide what is best for his children. He produced the children. They belong to him much more than they belong to the 'state'. Unless he is declared 'unfit to be a parent' in a Court of Law, he claims the right to bring up his children with a minimum of interference from the state."[1]

The onslaught has been formidable, and has doubtless done something to encourage promiscuity among middle-class intellectuals, but the subversives are unduly optimistic when they suppose, as they sometimes seem to, that it has made any serious impression upon the solid mass of ordinary humanity.

"The Clever Ones told us before the war that family life was dying out. Yet all these ordinary men in camp with me regard the separation from their wives and children as their heaviest cross in the army. A man's dearest possession is the photograph of his wife and children. 'That's Muriel,' he says to me, 'with Bobby and Jean. . . . Yes, that's our back garden, and those are runner beans against the fence.' "[2]

Since the outbreak of war, the great evacuations have dealt another blow, whose effects cannot yet be estimated, to family life. Those who believe that regeneration is a condition of victory will welcome any activities, official or voluntary, which make for the welfare and cohesion of family life. They will desire to make an end of economic insecurity without encroaching too far upon the independence of the family.

[1] *A Soldier's New World* by Sapper D. H. Barber and Sapper M. Hollmes, 7.
[2] *Ibid.*, 2.

The other chief concern of those who believe that a Christian renaissance is necessary for our survival will be that it should be possible for all to feel a sense of purpose and vocation in their work. I shall not enlarge upon this subject here, since it is integrally connected with another of the three war-time perplexities, with which I am about to deal—Can a system which is part collectivist, and part individualist, generate industrial efficiency? Before, however, leaving the topic of the Christian revival which seems to be demanded of a nation fighting to preserve Christendom, I must say a word of the part of the Christian in politics. I believe that, whatever he may decide to do as a citizen or a politician, *as a Christian*, though he will hold strong views upon certain issues, he is not called upon to commit himself to a detailed political programme. It seems to me that upon many issues, including the major problem of industrial organisation, there need not be, and indeed cannot be, any one Christian view. Thus it is clearly possible for a Christian to believe either in Collectivism and the greatest possible measure of state control, or in Distributivism, and the greatest possible number of small businesses and small property owners. It is possible for a Lord Halifax and a George Lansbury, without ceasing to be sincere Christians, to hold mutually antagonistic views on most of the major political issues of the day. Wilberforce's circle, "the Saints" of "the Clapham sect," contained several Members of Parliament; all shared the same perfervid religious views, and would vote as one man when they considered that religious and moral issues were at stake, yet some were Whig and some Tory, and on ordinary political issues they would find themselves constantly at variance. Moreover Christians, *as Christians*, cannot possess the special knowledge which is necessary nowadays for the proper understanding of almost every political problem. I remember the pressure put on the Government at the time of the Japanese aggression in Manchukuo by worthy clerics and various Church organisations. It was the Christian duty of Britain, they said, to impose economic sanctions on Japan. Japan, they assumed, would infallibly submit to this peaceful pressure, there would be no war, Britain would have checkmated aggression, and all would be well. And all the time the British Government was being warned by its responsible advisers, that, if there were sanctions, Japan would go to war. And these were the men who, whether they were right or wrong in the conclusions they drew from it, alone had access to the full facts without which no responsible judgment could be formed. The Churchmen did not know the facts, and without the facts were surely not entitled to so categorical an opinion. The history of the last twenty years teems with examples of worthy and enthusiastic, but insufficiently informed, Church and Chapel men rushing in where angels might well have hesitated to tread. An illuminating example is quoted by Sir Alfred Zimmern: [1]

"In the early months of 1932 Mr. Ramsay MacDonald's Government was paving the way for an International Conference . . . to clear up finally the question of German reparations. For this purpose it was necessary to obtain the consent of the French Government, to whom the bulk of this German debt was due. Now, in the action which the British Government was taking there was a double motive. They desired to get rid of these German political debts because they thought it would be of advantage to Europe generally

[1] *Spiritual Values and World Affairs*, 3.

180

. . . secondly, because it would be of particular advantage to this country, and in this country to financial and industrial circles, since it would make it easier for Germany to pay her very considerable commerical debts to British creditors.   Thus the issue between Great Britain and France was not so much the abolition of reparations as whether political debts or commerical debts, that is to say, French debts or British debts, were to have priority.   Rather a delicate matter when it is remembered what the political debts represented to the French mind—four and a quarter years of enemy occupation of a considerable area of their country. Now, at this juncture, a group of gifted amateurs, including certain leading Anglicans and Free Churchmen, issued a manifesto, couched in religious—not to say sanctimonious—language in favour of the cancellation of all reparations 'by forgiveness,' backing up their appeal by a quotation from the Sermon on the Mount.   I call them gifted amateurs, because if they had been deliberately meditating sabotage they could hardly have hit on a course of procedure so likely to be damaging to their professed cause.   Imagine the effect of their statement in Paris, where, of course, it seemed clear evidence of the existence of a private wire between Church House, Westminster and the Bank of England. 'British hypocrisy.'   No, of course not.   It was only British ignorance. 'Fools rush in where angels fear to tread.' Yes, but when the fools profess to be ministering angels, is not their folly double-dyed?"

The business of Christians, *as Christians*, is to denounce the social evil, and to insist that the politicians must get rid of it—not to commit themselves in detail to one particular remedy.   Because they are Christians, they can say, "slums must be abolished", but though, if they choose they can also say, "a public housing corporation, floated on a public loan at three per cent, is the best means of abolishing them," this will not be because they are Christians. All this applies *a fortiori* to the organised Churches. The first business of the Churches is to make Christians, and if they should ever succeed in this, there will not be much need of other reforms. Meanwhile let them tackle whatever problems are to be found on their own parochial front doorsteps, and tell Parliament what national abuses need reforming, or where the measures it is hatching affront the consciences of Christians. It will be tempting, no doubt, to go further, to prove that they are up to date and this-wordly by framing comprehensive social programmes of their own, or by semi-officially committing themselves to this Party or the other. But they will be wise to stop short of this. For such activities they have no special commission or qualifications, and by undertaking them they will in several ways be hampering themselves in their own chief duty of making Christians.

It is always tempting to shout with a crowd, or to win the favour of the paramount power in the state, and now that the two processes have become identical, the Church should remember how in the past it has in turn supported the Tudors, the Stuarts, and the landed aristocracy of the eighteenth century. Perhaps what is needed, to bring Christian influence to bear upon politics, is rather some Christian Political Union, on the model of the League of Nations Union, bound to no one Party, but ready to exercise pressure on all, and intervening whenever Christian principles appear to be at stake. Nevertheless, without moral and spiritual revival there can be no political regeneration.

Never in our history has a spiritual revival been more needed. It is now literally a matter of life and death. And to whom should we look first, if not to the Churches? Nor is it quite so formidable a task as it may seem at first sight. War itself drives us back upon the simple, enduring substance of human life, and breaks terrifyingly in upon our careless self-sufficiency. We are ripe for a new experiment. If the Churches will not lead us, doubtless there are others who will. Everywhere (as my own postbag would be enough to assure me) there are men and women, aware how widely in the last hundred years we have gone astray, conscious that without regeneration we dare not hope for survival, and looking to the future, not for more comforts but for a better life.

"In a thousand parts of the country, little groups of people are talking of the new leaven which is at work. Soon the feeling will gather momentum. When we have suffered a few years more, it will steal through the towns and the villages, small streams falling into rivers on their way to a larger gathering. Laymen form the bulk of this uprising, and presently leaders will come to them as the most natural thing in the world. Only, this time, the leaders will *know*.

"The bonds of comfort and complacency will be snapped by the rising energy. The salt tang of the ocean, to which these streams will flow, will sharpen our appetite for living. Against our wills, and in spite of anguish for a dying and privileged past, we shall be battered and braced into experience."[1]

[1] Julian Duguid, *I am Persuaded*, 350-1.

§ 8

Another of the three current questions of which I
spoke above, in which our past history takes shape as our
present perplexities, was, Can we expect the greatest
possible efficiency from an economic system which is
part Collectivist, part Individualist? May we not be
getting the worst of both worlds? This, I suppose, is
roughly how the misgiving presents itself in war-time,
although when we think of the age after the war, we
shall wish to add, How far can such a system be expected
to provide the basis of the more moral society which we
hope to see?

I suspect that most people who think about such matters
at all suppose that there is a simple explanation of our
curious amalgam of Collectivism and Individualism,
state ownership, state control, state regulation, and
private enterprise and laisser-faire. Nineteenth-century
individualism, they would say, is steadily yielding place
to twentieth-century collectivism. We find ourselves
in a moment of transition, that is all. The change is
bound to proceed at an ever-quickening pace, and before
long the state will be everywhere and everything, much
as it is in Germany or Russia. And the almost unreason-
ing assumption that a vast increase of Collectivism now
lies in the logic of history can be reinforced by persuasive
arguments. How else can we compete with these modern
unitary states, in which each industry is a vast state-
regulated unit—how compete with them in either peace
or war? How can there be efficiency without planning,
or planning without state control? The case for the
maximum degree of state planning is put at its strongest

in one of the broadsheets issued by a group which calls itself Political and Economic Planning.

"Salisbury (XIIIth century) and Bath (XVIIIth century) are at least as English as Liverpool and Slough, only they happen to have been planned. Any one who reads *The Battle of Britain* will appreciate that only a highly complex system of planning in advance saved this country from becoming a Nazi province last autumn. Yet hit-or-miss methods which, if applied by the fighting forces, would clearly lead to instant defeat, still prevail in the activities upon which the fighting forces depend for their vital supplies, and in civil defence."[1]

We shall most of us be ready to accept the plea that industry and organisation must be efficient. And if we ask, Efficient for what? the answer will be, no doubt, For production; for production in war, certainly, and not less for production in peace—for it should be observed that the oft-repeated dictum that the problem of production is solved, and that it only remains to solve the problem of distribution, is a myth ; the problem of production is very far from solved. Our economic organisation certainly presents a curious picture, recalling the famous passage in which Burke compares a Coalition Government to a tessellated pavement. Even the various activities of the state which one might have expected to find conforming to a few clear types, are of bewildering variety. There is that public ownership and control, as of the Post Office, which at the beginning of the century was the ideal of almost all Socialists for almost all industries. There is the condominium between the state

[1] *Planning*, No. 173, July 15, 1941.

and local public authorities which appears, for example, in the elementary schools. There is the Public Corporation, such as the B.B.C., where the state owns and supervises, but does not control. And (even in peace-time) there is such a Daedalian maze of wage boards, price boards, production boards, checks, controls, licences, regulations and subsidies that few indeed are the pies in which the state does not have at least one finger, and the most industrious bureaucrat can hardly be familiar with more than a fraction of either pies or fingers. Nor when one turns to privately owned industry and independent, voluntary associations, does the variety of type appear to be any less extensive and perplexing. At one end of the scale, and nearest, in one sense, to the borderline of Collectivism, comes the huge, privately owned trust or monopoly, at the other the village one-man business. Between, is a vast range of types and sizes. Finally, in every town and village in the land there are the countless independent and self-governing voluntary organisations, from the Boy Scouts or the Mothers' Union to the village slate club, all of which in a unitary state would be either state-controlled or extinct. Are all private and voluntary activities, eventually, by the familiar political doctrine of inevitability, the prolonging of the line AB, to surrender to the state? Few, I imagine, would go quite so far as this. The Planning broadsheet which I have just quoted pronounces merely that we should openly adopt the conception of government as the nation's common instrument for expanding its social and economic welfare in all those spheres where individuals or private associations cannot achieve equally effective results. Exactly, but which *are* these spheres? And who is to decide which they are, Government or governed? Let us for a moment take a bird's-eye conspectus of the industrial and social activities which are still, normally, uncontrolled by the state.

In production, the large-scale unit, in some form or other, is now inevitable. In the making of goods which are specialised or of exceptional quality there will always be room, and, it is to be hoped, increasing room, both for small manufacturers and hand workers, but for better or worse this is the age of mass production, and in any-thing like mass production the large unit has unrivalled advantages. All the same, the great private trust or monopoly is an equivocal phenomenon. It may often be more enterprising than a state department; its officials, for one thing, can be sacked. In general, however, to be a subordinate in a vast sub-department of Imperial Chemical Industries cannot be very unlike being a sub-ordinate in a Ministry of State—with the difference that one may happen to remember that, behind all the vast creative activity, and the obvious service to the public, in the last resort one is working to enrich a number of anonymous shareholders. And this is the sort of reflection which may sometimes rob a man of that sense of purpose and dignity in industry to which he has a right, and without which any system must be regarded as immoral. A man will face hardship and sacrifice for the com-munity, for an idea, for a faith, in peace as well as war, but he cannot be expected to face hardship and sacrifice for somebody else's profits, particularly when that some-body else is an anonymous shareholder who represents that most dubious of principles, ownership without responsibility. Moreover the wealth which can be accumulated by the captains and creators of great private industrial concerns is grotesque and shocking. Lord Nuffield may have originated a new industry, and it would be difficult indeed to make a more splendid use of great riches than has Lord Nuffield; nevertheless the community might reasonably have expected to obtain, and often has obtained, services as valuable as Lord Nuffield's for an insignificant fraction of their reward. Does any man deserve more than the salary of a Prime Minister? And however discreetly and self-sacrificingly it is used, great wealth must bring its owner excessive power; for if he chooses, he can buy power with it; and even if he gives it away, his most unselfish benefactions may redirect the development of great national institutions, and so become in fact the exercise of power. And sometimes the vast rewards go not so much for service as for actual injury to the state. Millions have been made by speculative builders, who may sometimes have run up houses more quickly and cheaply than the public authority, but have covered thousands of acres with mean and hideous caricatures of what a home should be, a glaring—though not, probably, in most cases, a very lasting—testimony to ignorance and greed.

In distribution, the vaster organisations, chain store, department store or emporium, are less prepossessing than in production. These, too, have of course the various economic advantages of mere size, but in two special ways they are less agreeable to the ordinary citizen. For one thing, as customer, he comes into direct personal contact with the great store, as he does not with the great factory, and he is apt to find them too impersonal for his taste. Moreover, though the small man cannot open a factory he can keep shop himself, so that the great store may become his most formidable rival.

As to the small individual concern, though it may have a diminishing place in production, there is likely always to be room for the firm which turns out specialised or high-quality goods, as well, it is to be hoped, as for the firm in which the employer still knows the employed as individual human beings. As in the large concerns the owners may receive an excessive reward for their services, whatever they may be, to the community; all that can be said is that the rewards are hardly capable of reaching the same colossal scale, and that they are likely more frequently to be earned by enterprise or the taking of risks. The same moral problem, of the worker without sufficient motive, may be there, but will probably be mitigated by less monotonous work and more personal contacts.

In distribution we know the economic defects of the small business—a smaller range of goods, in all likelihood somewhat higher prices, more antiquated methods —but the war has reminded us forcibly of some of its human virtues. It is one thing to queue up in the chain store, and be served by a harassed and anonymous assistant, complete with uniform overalls and metal number-badge, who slaps down our cheese, and turns wearily to Next Please, and quite another to shop at Robinson's round the corner, where old Mr. Robinson is sure to inquire if there is any more news of Dick, who is with his regiment in the Middle East, and will remember that Bobbie is home for his holidays and has a particular weakness for cherry cake, and will keep a surreptitious fifty Gold Flakes for the week when we are expecting the cousins whose house has been bombed.

The voluntary organisations, the third main element in the patchwork of private enterprise, are the vital arteries of a democratic society. Thanks to Wilberforce and the Abolitionists, who invented the technique of peaceful political propaganda, for more than a century this country has been covered by a network of Societies for Promoting this, that and the other, and almost the same number of Societies for Opposing them. It is thus that its life blood circulates in the political structure. If politics merely meant Parliament, Parliament would have perished long ago of pernicious anæmia. Nor, of course, is it by any means only the promotion of (or resistance to) the sort of object which can be furthered in Parliament that keeps hundreds of thousands of energetic citizens busy, out of working hours, as chairmen, treasurers, secretaries, committee men or merely persistent and argumentative members of countless Societies, Associations and Movements. These are the men and women who have kept British democracy alive when a score of imitations, which did not, or could not, imitate this particular quality, have perished. When some years ago the Olympic Games were held in Germany, and a number of Members of the British Parliament visited that country, as official guests, they were vividly impressed, not to say alarmed, by the ubiquitous evidence of the great state-organised drive for physical fitness then in full swing in Germany. As they watched the endless columns of bronzed young athletes, more than one of the visitors registered a silent vow that something of the sort must speedily be initiated in Britain. They returned chafing at the thought of our shameful inertia, and resolved to launch a rival British campaign immediately. When, however, they were able to look into the matter more closely, they began to discover, much to their astonishment, that although there had never been anything remotely resembling a state-organised drive for physical fitness in this country, there was scarcely a village in the country without its branch of one of the numerous, unco-ordinated voluntary organisations which, in their own enthusiastic, amateur way, were pursuing precisely this object. There were thousands of them—from the Women's League of Health and Beauty to the local troop of Boy Scouts or the physical jerks squads on the roof-gardens of London department stores. There was overlapping, no doubt, and waste of effort, and not so many citizens were affected as might have been caught up in a vast, more or less compulsory, state drive, but the whole affair was friendly and spontaneous and enthusiastic and *alive*. And so we begin to see a picture of a society which may be less efficient than a state despotism, but is more independent; which may be a good deal less highly trained, but is a good deal more flexible; a society in which men are not robots, as in Germany, and do not fear responsibility, as in France; a society, in brief, in which there is character and individuality. Industry and organisation, we said, must be efficient. But efficient for what? For production, no doubt. And that is one of the several reasons why public enterprise is indispensable. But we begin to see that private enterprise, too, can claim its efficiency; only it is efficiency of another sort. The survival of the small-scale here and there in our tessellated pavement serves, too, to soften some of the asperities of life. Willie used to be driven to school each morning in the solitary village bus, and when he left his satchel behind in it, on the return journey, as he sometimes did, the proprietor would make a special detour, on his next trip, to leave the satchel at Willie's house, or perhaps send his son up on a bicycle. Now that the village bus has been superseded by a huge Transport Service, Willie reaches school, perhaps, more punctually, for which he is not particularly grateful, but when he wants to reclaim his satchel, as he still sometimes does, he has to fill up a form in an office in the county town.

A curious picture indeed, our tessellated pavement. A great deal of what is large-scale and impersonal, partly under public and partly under private control, and interlocked with a great deal of what is small-scale and individual, each method at its best capable of its own distinctive type of efficiency, each in varying degrees presenting the same moral problems. In the experience of the general public, as day by day consumers of goods and services, the contrast is probably not so sharp between public and private ownership as between the great enterprise, however owned and controlled, and the small. Thus the following passage from that soldiers' pamphlet [1] which I have quoted before, though true enough of the ordinary man's feelings towards state control, is probably almost equally true of his feelings towards really large-scale private enterprise.

"We look with mixed feelings upon large schemes of Nationalisation. Such things as coal and gas and electricity, iron and steel—yes. But when it comes down to taking away the cheery tobacconist from whom we buy our 'Special Blend' and substituting a sort of Post Office-tobacconist, we are quite sure we don't want that. Who ever got a tip for the 3.30 from a Post Office? Or was the Post Office interested when the wife had her second? In things that touch our daily life we do not want State Control. We would sooner, even, have the choice of six bad tea-shops to take the wife to on a Saturday, than have to go to one State-controlled good one. As for the pubs, the idea of a National Mark beer would entirely destroy our thirst. In brief, we believe that the state should be the servant of the individual, and not his master."

A Soldier's New World by Sapper D. H. Barber and Sapper M. Hollmes.

And so there are, in effect, two problems. Firstly, up to what point should large-scale enterprise supersede the small concern? And secondly, ought the large-scale enterprise to pass out of private ownership and control altogether? The two questions are obviously interrelated, for, unless we are satisfied with the way in which large-scale industry is organised, we are not likely to wish to see it extended further.

What are the true objects of industry and commerce? Presumably they are the same as the objects of all activities within the state—the moral and physical well-being of all its citizens. As far as industry is concerned, this must mean, for one thing, efficient production, which is to say production which satisfies the consumer by putting on the market at a just price an adequate quantity of honest, serviceable and seemly goods. But it must also mean an intelligible and honourable system of production, in which the worker can serve with as much moral satisfaction to himself as can the soldier in the army, or the doctor in the hospital.

Our war experience alone should have been enough to make it clear that nowadays there can be no efficient production without some central mechanism for the survey and direction of industry as a whole, and that this can only be in the hands of the state. However well organised separate industries may be, industry as a whole obviously cannot be expected to function effectively, unless somebody, somewhere, is in a position to organise the mutual relations of its separate parts, to decide, as we are accustomed to say in war-time, on priorities. At the particular moment at which I am writing, for example, no single British industry can contribute satisfactorily to the total war effort unless somebody has decided whether our eventual, supreme effort is to be on land or in the air, whether or not it is our intention one day to invade the Continent, whether aeroplanes, tanks or ships are what we need most. Our prospective shortage of coal must have been due to the lack of just this central supervision and direction. War, of course, is not an altogether reliable analogy. It is true that the Battle of Britain must have been won by supremely excellent planning in advance, but it does not follow that we ought to plan to the same extent everywhere and always, for the simple reason that the civilian will not stand being ordered about to the same extent as the soldier. If he would, we could solve unemployment—and establish the servile state—at a blow.

All the same, the waste of effort through lack of co-ordination extends almost everywhere. Research workers often investigate kindred subjects without being so much as aware of each other's existence—in the sphere of Politics, at least, this is certainly true; in the more exact sciences things may perhaps be better managed. It is part, no doubt, of the price which we pay for personal liberty, and the independence of our numberless voluntary organisations. But there seems no reason why we should pay it. Voluntary organisations, and even industries under private ownership and control, are quite compatible with central powers of supervision and co-ordination in the hands of the state. No doubt the existence of such a central authority would mean that no one industry could be completely independent; the framework within which it must operate, its degree of "priority," would be determined for it. But there is nothing intrinsically impossible in the combination of general state supervision of the whole field of production, combined with the private ownership and management of separate industries. The general control of education

by the state, which leaves much autonomy to local
authorities, suggests an analogy, and in fact this must
have been more or less the state of affairs to which Mr.
MacDonald's administration looked forward when it set
up an Economic Advisory Council, which it is said in
fact to have consulted extremely seldom. The real danger
of central state control is always that there may so easily
be too much of it. The range of efficiency of modern
communications causes an avalanche of information and
inquiries to descend upon the desk of civil servant and
Minister alike. They do what they can; the civil servant
passes on some of the papers to other civil servants,
equally snowed under; the Minister, pitilessly pursued
by "pouches," by night as well as day, eventually either
ignores them altogether or becomes an overdriven hack,
without leisure or resilience for the two or three important decisions a week which are his real business.
This is one reason why the Government cannot manage
industries itself. If it is to map the general course, and
plan the priorities, for industry, it must be left as free as
possible of responsibility for the details.

Further, if production is to be efficient, it is already
clear that a great deal of it will have to be large-scale
production. But what type of large-scale production?
Here the second element in the objects of properly organised production becomes relevant; it must be an intelligible and honourable system of production, in which
the worker can serve with as much moral satisfaction to
himself as can the soldier in the army, or the doctor in
the hospital. Like them, the worker in the factory
should feel that he is there, not to enrich anonymous
shareholders, or to earn as high a wage as possible, but
to serve some purpose beyond himself, which is abundantly worth serving. We can scarcely conceive the

soldier or the doctor striking for less work or more pay. "The miner's aim is to paralyse the mine when and as he pleases" (Mr. G. D. H. Cole); "the workers have the right to use every method likely to weaken the power of their employers" (Mr. W. Mellor); we can scarcely conceive such motives as these being attributed to Medicine or the Army. And not because doctors and soldiers are more unselfish human beings than riveters or miners, but simply because their whole conception of their work is necessarily different; the doctor and the soldier, and for that matter, numberless men and women in other callings, naturally think of themselves primarily as *serving*, and not as earning a wage. And if we were to compile a list of all those whose work may be called *service*, because they are fully conscious in it of a purpose beyond themselves, we should find, I fancy, that it consisted either of members of some organisation which does not work for profit—hospital nurses, schoolmasters, lifeboatmen, civil servants, clergymen—or else of those —railwaymen, for example—who, although employed by a profit-making undertaking, are brought into such close contact with the public that they are specially conscious of their personal responsibilities to it. What matters is the consciousness of service willingly given in some sufficient cause, whether the cause be represented by a great public institution or a solitary individual. Without it, the career of the stockbroker, however profitable, brings neither honour nor contentment; with it, the drudgery of the domestic servant, however ill-paid, can be both satisfying and dignified. I can remember some high-minded friends of mine insisting that their domestic servants should always sit down to meals with them. There was no reason why the plan should not have worked well, though, in fact, I seem to remember, in

196

this particular instance, it did not; but the notion that, without some such Cophetua gesture, domestic service is necessarily humiliating seemed to imply a perverted conception of that, and all, work. Only work badly done, or done in an unworthy cause, can be degrading. The contagion of profit, however, does very often infect the worker with a sense of frustration and resentment, which he would never feel if the object of his work were morally satisfying. Not by any means always; it is an absurd exaggeration to speak as if profit were always and every-where unnecessary and degrading. Economically it is useful, at any rate, in the earlier stages of an industry, as an incentive to risk. And where it is not an incentive, as with the staff of an industry owned by anonymous shareholders, its contagious effects are often neutralised. For an official in a responsible post the creative aspects of his work will overshadow the fact that he may be doing it to earn a profit for unknown persons. And an owner or employer who is working for his own profit is often much more conscious that he is building up an organisa-tion, or providing the community with some new form of service, than that he is piling up a bank balance. Even with the receiver of profits for whom profits come first and foremost, their effects may sometimes be partially sterilised by his thinking of himself as earning them for his wife and children. It is for the rank and file, the doers of monotonous, subordinate and impersonal tasks, which cannot in themselves provide working life with a suffi-cient motive, that profit as the motive of industry spells frustration and resentment, standing between them and the moral satisfaction of labouring for the general good. No industrial system in which there was not some deep-seated moral malady could have bred conflict and bitter-ness over so long a period that, by a final paradox, the public has actually come to regard the strike (and its more unfamiliar counterpart the lockout) as a normal phenomenon.

And of this malady it is clear that one of the chief causes is the existence of so large a quantity of functionless property, in the hands of shareholders whose ownership involves no obligation whatever—so that a man may own a third of a factory without so much as being aware whether it manufactures biscuits or buttons. This principle of functionless property, organised in the limited company and the trust, was, for practical purposes, the invention of the nineteenth century individualists, and ever since it made its appearance it has been denounced as the source of most economic evil by the enemies of *laisser-faire*, Conservative and Socialist alike. It was the first theme of the young Disraeli, the Disraeli of that Young England which was in fact an attempt to revive the central doctrines of the older England. "The tenure of property should be the fulfilment of duty," such was his constant theme. This salutary principle, he insisted, had been obliterated by the rise of the middle class, who had not made "a corresponding advance in the exercise of the great social duties." [1] Disraeli had put his finger on the fundamental evil early indeed. "When I see masses of property raised in this country which do not recognise that principle . . . when I hear of all this misery and all this suffering . . . I cannot help suspecting that this has arisen because property has been permitted to be created and held without the performance of its duties." [2] This doctrine, preached by Disraeli's Young England Tories in 1840, is indistinguishable in essence from the theme of one of the most per-

[1] Speech in the Chartist Debate, 1839.
[2] Speech at Shrewsbury, 1843.

suasive works of modern Socialist propaganda, Mr. R. H. Tawney's *Acquisitive Society*. Indeed until Socialism, which historically has nothing to do with class, was appropriated, at the end of the last century, as the political philosophy of the rise of the wage-earners (as Individualism had served as the political philosophy of the rise of the middle class) it was often scarcely distinguishable from Tory democracy, both being bitter attacks upon *laisser-faire* and the illusion of the Economic Man. Thus it was perfectly natural that Lord Goderich, for example, in the eighteen forties, should be, at one and the same time, both a Conservative Member of Parliament, one of the Disraelian Tories of Young England, and also a member of the Christian Socialist group led by Maurice and Kingsley. It is true that, although Disraeli was responsible for some of the most bitter and illuminating comments ever made upon this nineteenth-century conception of an ownership which owes no duty, he did not do very much to end it. But then by the time Disraeli first attained power, as distinct from office, in the 'seventies, not only was he an old man, but the wealthy middle class, the embodiment of the new and meaner idea of property, had begun to move rapidly out of the old Whig Party, now turning Gladstonian Liberal, into the new Conservative Party, which Disraeli led. And as late as 1870 he could still insist (in the preface to the first Collected Edition of his novels) that "the main principle of the feudal system, that the tenure of property should be the fulfilment of duty, is the essence of good government." The first Labour Socialists, in the 'nineties, though few of them were disciples of Marx, were inclined to attack all property as such, and indeed by that time functionless shareholding had spread so fast and far that there was some justification for an indiscriminate attack.

But ever since, there have been thoughtful Socialists, such as Mr. Tawney, who have fastened upon functionless property, the principle of privilege without obligation, as the chief source of the distemper of modern industry. There are thus powerful and respectable precedents, in both the largest political camps, for an attack upon the principle of functionless shareholding. And viewed in this light, it is clear that the large, privately owned industry is quite incapable of overcoming this fundamental moral defect, since it possesses neither of the possible psychological antidotes, neither bringing its employees into close personal contact with their public, as it might if it were not large, nor naturally putting the needs of the community first, as it might if it were not privately owned.

And now it is necessary to recall that common assumption that, in the pattern of industry also, the familiar process of prolonging the line AB is necessarily at work, and that we find ourselves midway in a now inevitable transition from complete *laisser-faire* to complete state control. Both elements in this assumption are false. There never has been complete *laisser-faire* in Britain, and it is improbable that there will ever be complete state-control. During the last two decades, however, there has appeared a succession of specimens of a quite new type of industrial organisation, the Public Corporation, of which the best known is the British Broadcasting Corporation. Other conspicuous examples are the Port of London Authority, created by a Liberal Government in 1909, the Central Electricity Board, set up by a Conservative Government in 1926, and the London Passenger Transport Board, first projected by a Labour administration, and actually established by the National Government in 1933. The Public Corporation, which has long been approved by Socialist theory, and is indeed a Socialist invention, is thus far from being the exclusive patent of any one school or Party, and may be said to represent ground common to all of them in the instinctive desire to steer between the Scylla of rigid state bureaucracy and the Charybdis of unbridled private enterprise. It cannot, of course, be assumed that the middle course will be more effective, simply because it is a middle course. Only, it is clearly very much more *possible*. For the choice between Scylla and Charybdis implies in fact a choice between, on the one hand, the conscription of labour by the state and, on the other, a much wider distribution of private property. The conscription of labour would no doubt solve many problems, including, of course, the problem of unemployment, but it would not be tolerated by British wage-earners, and could hardly be administered by a Parliamentary system, which indeed may have been why the pamphlet-programme of the Socialist League in 1932 and 1933 contemplated the transfer of the powers of Parliament and Cabinet to a Party Directorate on the Nazi-Communist model. A much wider distribution of property, on the other hand, is undoubtedly a highly moral conception, but our economic integration has advanced far beyond the point at which a community of industrial and agricultural small proprietors is conceivable, without changes even more revolutionary than those which would be needed to establish conscription of labour; nor could a community so organised hope to compete effectively with the unitary systems of to-day. In contrast with these extreme alternatives, the public corporation is a natural outcome, instead of a violent distortion, of our recent development, and is moreover both compatible with Parliamentary Government and capable of competition with its formidable contemporary rivals. What, then, are its chief attractions?

Details differ in the specimens already in existence, but there are certain essential features, most characteristically represented in the B.B.C. The B.B.C. is a monopoly owned by the state, and its surplus income goes to swell the public revenue; thus the profit motive has been eliminated, and the employees of the Corporation naturally think of themselves as directly serving the community. The state, through the Postmaster-General or (in wartime) the Minister of Information, is responsible for its long-term policy, but hands over its day-to-day administration to a Board of Governors appointed by itself. Thus, while it is possible for the state to fit broadcasting into the general pattern of national policy, the Corporation has for practical purposes all the sense of freedom and personal responsibility natural to an independent undertaking. Its staff is paid on a scale somewhat higher than the civil services, and somewhat lower than the employees of private businesses. Civil servants have become traditionally more or less irremovable, partly because, if they could be easily got rid of, there would be a temptation to the successive politicians who are their temporary masters to dispose of those whom they suspected of political tendencies inconvenient to themselves. The service of the Corporation, over which politicians have no direct authority, is not, like the service of the Government, virtually a life appointment, and this is doubtless one of the reasons why it has always seemed to display considerably more liveliness and enterprise than a Government department. Its service to the public compares favourably with that of privately owned and competitive undertakings. It has contrived to combine, on the whole with astonishing success, the apparently incompatible obligations of educating the public taste and giving the listener what he wants, satisfying a vast majority of its enormous public, without sinking to the level sometimes reached by the commercialised popular Press and the competitive, privately owned broadcasting systems of the United States. Occasionally, in war-time at anyrate, there have been faint suggestions of excessive political interference, the banning, for example, of a popular performer because he, or she, happened to be politically *persona non grata* to some incoming ministerial influence; but that the rival political creeds have on the whole been dealt with impartially seems to be established by the unanimous conviction of every Party, expressed to the Ullswater Committee in 1935, that its opponents had been treated more generously than itself, and the subsequent conclusion of the Committee that none of these complaints was justified. For those who do the actual broadcasting, a Corporation is doubtless far less profitable than a private company. In the United States a popular broadcaster earns huge sums, and becomes a popular institution. In Britain he is paid comparatively insignificant fees, and unless he has an independent public in the theatre or the concert hall, is discarded as soon as he establishes a reputation. But for the *consumer*, the general public, which is after all what matters, there can be no doubt that the Corporation gives better service than the private enterprise.

On the whole, the record of the B.B.C. certainly commends this new conception of a utility service, publicly owned, subject only in the last resort to Parliamentary control, carrying its own risk and managed on business lines. This is not to say that all industry should be uniformly organised on the pattern of the Public Corporation. The supply of electricity and the supply of

socks imply very different problems and may demand
very different organisations. But there is at the least
by now a very good case for extending the Public Corporation over considerable areas of industry, a process
which should keep legislators busy for about as long as
any one concerned with the foreseeable future, and not
with paper Utopias, need at present concern himself.
Certain principles can be laid down as to this extension.
In the first place, no economic function ought to be permanently maintained as a parasite upon others. This
would mean the removal from tax-maintained municipal
authorities, and so from support by the public purse, of
such gas, electricity, transport and other undertakings
as they at present control, and their transfer to Public
Corporations. There would be a further advantage in
this change, apart from the ending of much economic
parasitism. The municipality, after all, is *ex hypothese* a
small and homogeneous area, and the attempt to cramp
the operation of public utility services into it is manifestly
breaking down. Sometimes, though by no means always,
the municipality stands to gain by its narrow limits;
electricity, for example, can be distributed more cheaply
in a town than in the countryside, but, in the national
interest, the town should bear its share of the extra cost
of serving less populous areas, just as, thanks to a world-
wide organisation, it costs the same to post a letter from
the Highlands to Australia as from Westminster to
Kensington. The erection of a national grid for gene-
rating and carrying electricity is a spectacular admission
of this principle, but it is a principle which applies
equally to gas, water, docks and railways, to various
forms of road transport, and probably to mines. There
is no defence for covering the country with a national
network of pylons carrying 132,000 volts, and then

leaving the distribution of all this energy to an obsolete system of uneconomic areas and conflicting ownerships. So far, these changes will mean in general the transfer of industries from one form of public control, mainly that of local authorities, to another, that of the Public Corporation, and to many this will seem superfluous, since the unreflecting commonly suppose that once an industry has been subjected to some form of public ownership or control, no matter what, and so long as private profit is to some extent curbed, all problems have been finally solved. As to which I cannot do better than quote the authors of *Planning*: [1]

> "Much mischief has been caused by this crudely polit-ical view, which continues in favour in many quarters, although the best minds in all Parties now recognise that it is more important to get low-cost power or low-cost transport, with imaginative and reliable service and decent conditions for those rendering it, than to have the privilege of voting once a year for the man who, if elected, will support the man who, if put on the right committee, will have a nineteenth part of a decisive voice in choosing the manager of the local electricity or transport undertaking."

But outside the whole field of local authority, there seems no obvious reason why great industries which, by eliminating domestic competition, have reached an advanced degree of integration—the great soap and chemical trusts, the great chocolate and tobacco combines—should not be transformed into public utility corporations. And there are numerous industries already well on the road to a high degree of unification which might

[1] No. 5, June 20, 1933.

be speeded through its final stages, and then similarly remodelled. But of both these fields it is necessary to speak with caution and humility. Nothing is easier, or more tempting, than to frame sweeping generalisations about whole categories of industry with whose very various individual problems no layman can have more than a nodding acquaintance. Here the empirical advance is essential. First we accept the view that the Public Corporation is in theory a desirable pattern for the integrated industry, and then we ask whether, having regard to all the circumstances, it is desirable to remodel this particular industry in this particular way at this particular moment. Moreover, let it be repeated once again that any industrial system whatever which is worked by practising Christians will be superior to any industrial system whatever which is managed by selfish materialists. After making these reservations, I can only record my own present belief that for a great unified, or almost unified, industry management by a Public Corporation at its best would be both more moral and more efficient than management by a private trust or combine, or by such modified competition as might survive between one or two powerful interests. It should mean more contented employees, no excessive fortunes, a readier response to national interests, and a closer adjustment to the framework of national policy as a whole. It should deliver industry from the poison, at its two extremes, of those who believe that industry exists not for the consumer but for themselves—those owners for whom "a good year" means a year of high profits, and those wage-earners whose ideal of "the mines for the miners" I remember hearing warmly endorsed by a gathering of young Socialist intellectuals. I should like also to think that it might lead in time to such a considerable rise in wages at the expense of profits (never so likely in privately owned industry) as might eventually carry considerable numbers of employees outside the range of direct dependence upon the social services altogether. For I believe that there is beginning to be real moral danger in the habit of looking to the state as the universal provider of material comforts, as school-master, nurse, guardian and rich godparent combined, as the taker of all important decisions and the shelter against all possible risks. It is a habit acquired for the most part during the vast expansion of the social services since the last war, and now very widely diffused. An incomplete calculation showed that in the year 1931-32 not less than twenty-two million British citizens, or about half of the total population, were receiving some support from the state (the total cost of eight of the principal relief services being then about £320,000,000, or one-twelfth of the entire national income). There was undoubtedly an unpleasant dash of hypocrisy and harsh-ness about the way in which Victorian individualists, who recognised virtually no responsibility for the poor, constantly exhorted them to cultivate enterprise and self-reliance. But for all that, enterprise and self-reliance remain major virtues, and there was beginning to be an un-welcome suggestion of materialism and decadence about the contrary view, so popular of late, that what matters most are not a citizen's services, but his needs, not his duties, but his rights. The decline of enterprise and self-reliance among factory workers, though those who know them well can hardly fail to notice it, is not yet serious or deep-rooted, and may be largely due to the deadening character of factory work. But then the British are hereditarily enterprising and self-reliant, and it would take generations for the germ of inertia and dependence to make serious inroads upon their native virtues. The fact remains that there are signs that the germ is at work, and also that it is partly at any rate due to the assumption by the state of so many of the responsibilities which would normally fall to the lot of the husband or parent. This is a tendency against which the average Briton will rebel, when he recognises it, although more often the "mental climate" will prevent him from being aware of its existence.

"The Ordinary Man demands the *means* to give his son a long education, but he claims the right to decide what is best for his children. He produced the children. They belong to him much more than they belong to the ' State.' Unless he is declared ' unfit to be a parent ' in a Court of Law, he claims the right to bring up his children with a minimum of interference from the State." [1]

This is undoubtedly a widespread view, and although those who hold it may often unconsciously be wishing to have it both ways, both to receive full benefits and to retain full independence, it certainly deserves consideration. At this point I wish only to indicate that, thanks to greater economies and lower profits—and indeed even perhaps without them, since the state would save by reduced social services—the Public Corporation should be able to pay higher wages, and, that being so, it might be possible, while actually increasing the prosperity of large numbers of citizens, to remove the slow threat to human personality of excessive dependence upon the state. The state would shape the pattern and direct the energies of industry, but it would not encroach so constantly and directly upon the individual life.

[1] Sapper D. M. Barber and Sapper M. Hollmes, *A Soldier's New World*, 7.

Another effect would follow from the spread of Public Corporations, using their profits to increase wages and swell the revenues of the state. Great industrial fortunes would begin to disappear, removed not partially and indirectly by taxation, but completely and directly from the source. And so the whole aspect of taxation would begin to change. At present taxation is treated as a means of redistributing wealth, by way of a subvention, through the social services, to the inadequate wages paid by industry. The captain of industry is shorn of some of his profits, to assist the state to swell the low wages which helped to make his profits possible. But not the captain of industry only. The earners of fixed salaries, who, unlike the captain of industry and the wage-earner, can make no adjustment in their earnings to meet high taxation, also make their contribution to the real incomes of the wage-earners, and in doing so no doubt suffer a greater economic strain than the millionaire, so that taxation which is thought of as penalising the profit-maker, in fact probably penalises the earners of salaries first and foremost. When more and more citizens earn fixed salaries for services rendered, and fewer receive large, fluctuating and unpredictable profits, when a larger share of the proceeds of industry goes direct to the wage-earner as earnings, and not indirectly as assistance received from the state, when a larger proportion of the cost of the social services is contributed by those who benefit from them, taxation will have to shift towards consumption instead of profit, and its whole nature will have been transformed.

Somewhat less-developed industries, in which integration has advanced some way, but needs to go further, are not likely to be left entirely to themselves. Since most well-developed industries are themselves anxious for further unification, and since the only promising alternative to Government control is voluntary action under powers devolved by Parliament, a likely course is the passing of an Enabling Act for particular industries, or indeed for industry as a whole. The passing of such an Act would be optional for the industry concerned, but, once passed, it would be compulsory upon a recalcitrant minority within it. The Act would empower the industry to set up all, or any, of those common agencies whose creation an unenlightened minority can so often obstruct —regulation of output, sales and distribution; power to enforce amalgamation and eliminate redundancy; to arrange for welfare work and the training of personnel; to provide for common research, costing, statistics and publicity, and for standardisation of processes and products. Some of these powers would only be granted in return for a certain degree of public supervision in the interest of other industries, and of the consumer. Such methods would put an end to the power of the backward minority in an industry to obstruct technical progress and undermine wage rates and labour standards.[1] Industries which failed to make good use of these powers might be treated as inviting more drastic Government intervention.

In much less-developed industries, in which, for the time being, profits are still a valuable incentive to risk, I see, for my part, no present alternative to private enterprise. Or, to put it in another way, to prophesy as to these would be to look further ahead than the prime consequences and sequel of the war, the first stages of the highroad into the new age, which is all that a book such as this can profess to survey.

As for Distribution, despite all the plans for remodel-

[1] On an Enabling Act for Industry see e.g. *Planning*, Nov. 26, 1934.

210

ling the factory, there have so far been no serious plans for remodelling the shopping system—for the Co-operative Movement can hardly be called a plan. Perhaps the reason is that the shop-assistant, who comes into close personal contact with the public he serves, has never suffered from the spiritual *malaise* of the factory hand. Or perhaps it is because about seventy-five per cent of retail shops (it has been reckoned) are "family" shops, employing no one outside the owner's family. The reason certainly is not that distribution is so completely and intelligently organised already that it needs no improvement. It is not, as it should be in peace-time, a smoothly running two-way traffic, carrying to the producer accurate information as to what the consumer wants, and to the consumer the goods he needs at the lowest possible prices. On the contrary, the producer who has made sweeping improvements in the factory may see all his economies swept away by a wasteful retail system, whose excessive costs keep most of his goods out of the consumer's reach; while the consumer finds himself paying an increasing proportion of his purchase money to a retailer who too often, as far as he can see, does next to nothing in return for it. Thus, as an author, I do not object to seeing a third of the retail price of this book going to the bookseller, if the bookseller has earned it by keeping a copy of the book in stock, or, at the least, by being able to give the inquiring would-be purchaser elementary information about it; but I do resent a third going to the small stationer whose stock consists of a couple of hundred cheap detective novels, who has never heard of my book, and whose only service may be to take down particulars inaccurately at the dictation of the purchaser, and, after a week's unnecessary delay, dispatch an illiterate order to the publisher. But what is to be done about it? There are no serious plans, and not enough is known about the retail system for serious plans to be made. The war has reminded us of the friendly adaptability of the small retailers, and the rigours of war-time have concealed some of their shortcomings. On the other hand, the dearth of commodities, sometimes dexterously assisted by the manufacturer, has extinguished some of the smallest and least efficient altogether. Perhaps the answer is that eventually the industrial Public Corporations will step in (as certain well-organised privately owned industries have already begun to do) to organise their own distribution. Perhaps the well-organised chain stores and larger retail units will eventually control much of distribution under a charter of self-government, granted, on conditions, by the state. But the family shop, we may be sure, will be an unconscionable time in dying. It is uneconomical, unscientific and inefficient. But it is also friendly and accommodating; it creates small property owners; and it is highly individual. And are we not fighting this war to defend individuality?

As for the vast, heterogeneous network of voluntary organisations, the bulk of them, we may be sure, will persist. They are the richest and most typical expression of British vitality and individuality, and when they disappear Britain will be dying. Some, nevertheless, are bound to go, superseded by the state. For one thing, many national services have long been supported by private generosity, and very largely by the generosity of that great central class of receivers of fixed incomes which, as always, is bound to suffer most from rising prices and rising taxation. Sometimes from the platform at the annual meeting of some great voluntary national institution, such as the Royal National Lifeboat Institution,

I have observed the assembled subscribers, and reflected that probably seventy-five per cent of them depended on fixed incomes of between four hundred and a thousand pounds a year. The immense contributions made by these worthy folk, in voluntary service as well as cash, to scores of public causes is seldom allowed for by the economists who discuss the distribution of the national income; but such contributions cannot be expected in the future. Or consider the hospitals. There is much to be said, on purely technical grounds, for a comprehensive state medical service, and many of the war-time improvisations of the Ministry of Health are already laying its foundations. But the financial inconsistencies of the present system are alone enough to end it. It is an interesting and, in many ways, an admirable, example of the more or less unplanned dovetailing of older voluntary methods into the extending state activities of an age of Collectivism, but it belongs to an age which has passed. Apart from the few who can afford to pay for a private ward at a rate which means some profit to the hospital, its patients are either financed by public authorities or by voluntary insurance schemes to which they have themselves contributed small sums, such as a penny a week. The payments by the public authorities do not come anywhere near meeting the cost to the hospital of the patient's treatment; still less do the contributions of the insurance schemes. There is thus a gap, constantly increasing as prices rise, between the income of a hospital and its receipts, a gap which in theory is filled by the charity of prosperous subscribers, who are already helping to maintain the hospitals by paying their own doctors and surgeons the high fees which enable them to give free service in the public wards. Such is the theory; increasingly the practice is that hospitals live upon overdrafts. This is one more field in which mounting taxation alone is bound to extend the activities of the state, by the simple process of making the voluntary alternative impossible.

§9

There remains one more of those three questions, so often asked nowadays, which may be said to sum up the war-time perplexities which we inherit from our pre-war failings. Why does the Government hesitate to impose full economic sacrifices upon both the powerful and the many? Why not an Excess Profits Duty on *everybody*? It is the many just now who make the formidable problem. There are doubtless, as I have already suggested, plenty of owners and employers comfortably feathering their nests out of the war; but for the most part this will be in spite of the Government's policy, and not for lack of it. The Government has at any rate imposed an Excess Profits Duty of a hundred per cent. The Duty, and other official dealings with the profit-maker, may not be fully effective, but at least they represent a recognition that nobody ought to be richer for the war. At least there is an attempt to control profits, but there is no attempt to control wages. After a year of war the Government said that, despite the general rise in wages, there was no risk of inflation, and after nearly two years it said that there was. To that singularly unimpressive extent it has had something to say of the economic problem. But at no time has it had anything whatever to say of the moral problem. It has remained silent while wage-increases were claimed expressly on the ground that the wage-earner ought not to make any economic sacrifice in war-time. It has remained silent while Sir Walter Citrine, on behalf of the Trade Union Congress, protested against stabilisation of wages on the ground that this would mean that wage-earners "would be expected to accept a depressed standard of living for the rest of the war"—which is exactly what all the rest of the community is expected, and indeed exhorted, to accept. In a collection of *Notes for Speakers*, issued by the Ministry of Information, which lies beside me as I write, prospective orators are reminded that in the five months ending May, 1941, there was a net increase of about a million pounds a week in the wage rates of about 6,650,000 work people; that in the corresponding months of 1940 there were increases of £1,170,000 a week; and (in leaded type) that from the outbreak of the war to midsummer, 1941, wage increases amounted to nearly £4,000,000 a week. The brief, however, discreetly refrains from all comment; there are neither congratulations for the fortunate recipients, nor condolences for the less fortunate taxpayers who (since the Government will have bought a very considerable proportion of the goods whose cost has thus gone up by £4,000,000 a week) will eventually have to foot the bill. The Government knows well enough what the fighting forces say when they hear of a girl of nineteen with six months' experience earning five pounds a week, and deliberately and repeatedly late at work, whose shop steward threatens industrial trouble if she is sacked; it knows that the spectacular rise in industrial wages is now the chief social problem exercising men's minds all over the country; it knows these things because the regional officers of the Ministry of Information are reporting them regularly. But it continues to say nothing. In this way the Government has exposed itself to the criticism that, on the Home front, it is sometimes not so much a National administration representing the national interest, as a Coalition representing the more predatory instincts of both profiteer and wage-earner. And to even more far-reaching criticism than this. For in country after country it has been its reluctance to demand sacrifices of the masses which has sooner or later brought social democracy to destruction. All goes smoothly so long as all that is required is the sacrifices of the privileged few. But no state can maintain itself for ever, either morally or economically, upon the compulsory sacrifices of the few. And sooner or later the testing time must come: Is the people capable of voluntary sacrifice itself? In most of the states which have succumbed the answer, perhaps, might have been, Yes: what was lacking, it may be, was not moral fibre in the people, but moral courage in the politicians. The people was not asked for sacrifice. Be that as it may, the phenomenon has been disquietingly common. "The pathetic struggle in Spain, a struggle which M. Maritain described as a war between injustice and disorder, showed the inability of the Socialist to achieve co-operation and discipline when these demanded immediate sacrifices, not from a small privileged class but from the people themselves." [1] Mr. Bertrand Russell, in *Which Way Peace*, selected Denmark as the country whose future was most secure. An ascendant Socialism was concentrating upon prosperity; there was plenty of butter, and no guns. The conduct of the Danes, when the Germans struck, may, or may not, have been prudent, but it was certainly far from heroic. And to-day there is not even butter in Denmark. Up to now, September, 1941, the United States is still in danger of going down to history as a nation which loved comfort too long to face sacrifice when the

[1] Michael Roberts, *The Recovery of the West*, 87.

hour struck. As for us, though we have shouldered
sacrifices in plenty, are we free yet of the final risk—of
failing to shoulder the *complete* sacrifice, without which
we have no title to count on survival? How much
of our history in the last hundred years might almost
have been designed to ensure that we should flinch from
asking for economic sacrifice from the entire nation?
We have seen how the contagion of nineteenth-century
materialism spread from the profit-making employer to
the employed. So deeply rooted was illusion, that the
pursuit of self-interest came to be admired as a virtue,
and even identified with the principle of democracy itself.
"The most powerful influence," writes Mr. Delisle Burns
in his *Democracy*, "tending towards democracy was the
Trade Unions, *for the advancement of their own interests*;
this is real democracy." The italics are not Mr. Burns'.
Most of us are so accustomed to that natural consequence of profit-seeking materialism, the constant emphasis on rights and the constant neglect of duties, that
we even see nothing laughable in Mr. H. G. Wells'
Charter of *The Rights of Man*. And when Mr. Wells
solemnly lays down man's inalienable right to receive
nourishment, medical attention, and all the rest of it,
from his fellow-men, it scarcely occurs to us that the
"right" is meaningless, unless somebody else has acknowledged the corresponding duty—to provide his fellow-
men with nourishment, medical attention, and all the
other comforts catalogued by Mr. Wells. And yet all
history shows that men will respond to a call to self-
sacrifice far more readily than to a call to self-interest.
"I offer neither pay, nor quarters, nor provisions; I
offer hunger, thirst, forced marches, battles and death."
"I want the young men and women of America to dream
about the day when they will have a job that will enable

them to live in comfort and security." The two appeals do not proceed from the same moral universe. Garibaldi got his volunteers: did Mr. John L. Lewis? It may be said that to risk one's life is easier than to risk one's livelihood. But British citizens have proved over and and over again that, in a worthy cause, they will risk either. In 1931 a vast majority of citizens voted themselves a smaller income, because their leaders assured them that the sacrifice was necessary to avert national disaster; politicians "for the first time for many years, came to Westminster commissioned to offer their constituents' services to the nation, not to exploit the nation in their constituents' interests." [1] Who can doubt that to-day to the same appeal they would make the same response? But there must be an appeal. It is easy and tempting to hail sacrifices imposed on the few as "progress," and to denounce the suggestion that sacrifices should be accepted by the many as "reaction." But we are being tested for survival, and what is easy and tempting will not suffice. With money to be had for the asking, and all our leaders assuring us that we should be fools not to ask for it, nine out of ten of us will pocket the money, and be thankful. But with the same leaders urging us to sacrifice and service, nine out of ten of us will forget our pockets, and remember our duties. The very men who, in a profit-making factory, with its long tradition of high profits and wage-disputes, were ready to raffle their wage-packets, when there was less than ten pounds in them, would clamour, like their sons and brothers, for a chance to risk their lives for a few shillings, once they found themselves in the Royal Air Force with its long tradition of self-sacrifice. If we survive the war, and in the new age the Public Corporation, or some other

[1] Lord Eustace Percy, *Government in Transition*, 2.

form of organised service, begins to replace the profit-making industry, the tradition will root itself in industry, as it has rooted itself in the fighting forces and the professions. The trade union has been a great school of citizenship, teaching men to subordinate their private inclinations and opinions to a common policy, and transforming a mass of individuals into a disciplined brotherhood, but, like the public school, it has too often served narrowly class interests. When the motive of service replaces self-seeking throughout the whole hierarchy of industry, the trade union, like the public school, will be free to develop its virtues untrammelled by its vices, and we shall see the annual Trades Union Congress, for all the world like a conference of doctors or schoolmasters, devoting its attention to the technical problems of its service to the public, and not to the pay and prospects of its members.

All this, though it has suggested such a considerable transfer from private to public ownership, is far, I know, from presenting the picture of a uniform and logical system. But then I see no reason why a uniform and logical system should be either more desirable or more efficient. "Democracies should be sceptical of attempts to reduce the infinitely varied phenomena of politics and economics to a few sweeping general laws." [1] The compromise between extremes, the union of apparent incompatibles, the combination of state control with individual enterprise, is a natural outcome of our Parliamentary system, of a social tradition which is at the same time aristocratic and equalitarian, and, above all, of the national temperament. The compromise which already existed before the war was in many ways astonishingly effective. Deaths from the diseases which are the

[1] Lord Samuel, *Democracy.* The Herbert Spencer Lecture, 1941. 19.

surest symptoms of excessive poverty were declining to new low records, year after year; we were building a thousand houses a day; the weight and height of the elementary school-child was steadily rising.

"I lived most of those twenty years in East London, and I saw (despite left-wing statisticians, who are as unilluminating as their brothers of the Tory Party) a vast improvement in the health and education and living conditions of the people. There was much still left undone, but the progress was there. I saw it in clothes and complexions and food and houses and education and entertainment, and these things are realities, not theories." [1]

The standard of life of the ordinary man was probably higher in Britain than anywhere else in the world. In comparison with this the totalitarian states certainly had some social achievement to show, but, stripped of all their ballyhoo, they were not particularly impressive. In 1938 the income per head of the population in Russia, Italy and Japan had not reached the level passed by Britain in 1860.

Nevertheless it is still necessary to remember that *any* system worked by Christians will be preferable to *any* system controlled by materialists.

[1] Sapper D. H. Barber, *The Soldier's New Church*, 3.

VII

THE BRITISH NEW ORDER

§ I

When the news flashed round the world that Germany had struck at Poland, outside the British Commonwealth of Nations only France dared to challenge her. All the states of Europe were relatively near to the scene of the crime; and yet, save France (and indeed Russia, which, after applauding the aggression, moved in to share the spoils), not one of them stirred, while thousands of miles away, in Ottawa and Cape Town, Melbourne and Wellington, the British Dominions were pledging themselves to the struggle. All these passive states had subscribed to the Covenant of a League which solemnly bound them, by the most meticulous of paper constitutions, to resist aggression, yet not one of them stirred. No paper constitution, no legal fetters, bound the Dominions to Britain; the Canadians and South Africans, the Australians and New Zealanders were as free as Holland or Denmark to draw their skirts aside, and watch us risking everything alone. Nevertheless they fought. Between the collapse of France and the attack on Russia, the British Commonwealth alone stood between mankind and the return of barbarism; five hundred and twenty-five millions of human beings; a quarter of the earth's population, inhabiting a quarter of its surface. This is one of the revolutionary Facts of history, tremendous and inescapable. Nothing, not even our own folly, can now prevent its shaping the pattern of the age to come. When the war ends, no country save the British Commonwealth will have fought against Germany from beginning to end; perhaps no country then sharing in the struggle will have entered it of its own free will. Indeed facts such as these are fundamental. What are we to make of them?

§.2

Consider the three main elements of the British Commonwealth. The Dominions; a population of about twenty-two millions, and a habitable area of about six million square miles; "autonomous communities within the British Empire, equal in status, in no way subordinate one to another in any respect of their domestic or external affairs, though united by a common allegiance to the Crown, and freely associated as members of the British Commonwealth of Nations."[1] The core of the "first British Empire" had disappeared in 1783, with the secession of the United States. During the first thirty years of the reign of Victoria the acceptance of the new principle of responsible government for the chief Colonies, as they were then called, consolidated the "second British Empire." By 1914 Canada and Australia were federal states, and South Africa a Union of four Colonies. The British way of life had spread beyond Europe and was securely established in three more continents. This, in itself, is one of the great achievements of history. Much to the surprise of the Germans, the first German world war did not dissolve the British Empire. That war was followed, however, by what seemed to be a period of weakening ties. The symptoms were obvious enough. Thus the Dominions were separately

[1] Lord Balfour, at the Imperial Conference of 1926.

represented at the Versailles Conference of 1919, became separate members of the League of Nations in their own right, and were expressly excluded from the British guarantee of the Franco-German frontier in the Locarno Treaty of 1925. And in 1931 the Statute of Westminster recognised the plenary sovereignty of each Dominion Parliament, and disabled the British Parliament from legislating for any Dominion, unless at the express invitation of that Dominion's Parliament. Clearly formidable centrifugal forces were at work. At the end of the war a powerful reaction against the statesmen and the system which had apparently been responsible for the gigantic slaughter swept over the Dominions, and in 1922, when Mr. Lloyd George, in difficulties with Turkey, summoned the "united Empire" to his assistance, Canada replied coldly that war measures could not be taken without the assent of the Canadian Parliament, and that the Canadian Parliament was not in session. Material links were weakening too, as London ceased to be the financial centre of the world, and its control of credit began to disappear. The passing of the Statute of Westminster had been taken very calmly in this country, but it was not particularly easy to convince foreign observers, most of whom regarded it as the beginning of the end, and the most effective argument against the pessimists was the not entirely logical one that they had always been wrong before. The British Empire has almost always been upon the verge of dissolution, but it has not lost a colony since 1776. For one thing, pessimists, whose name has always been legion, both here and abroad, have overlooked many of the imponderabilia, such as the persistence of the British tradition in the Dominions.

"It is difficult to explain in hard words so ethereal an

entity as ' British traditions; ' yet one needs only to live in a British community, whether in England, Australia, or Canada, to see its reality. There is a peculiar attitude towards life and the world; there are certain manners and even mannerisms . . ." [1]

Moreover the threat of bankruptcy in 1931, and of the totalitarian states after 1935, produced a new cohesion and a new outbreak of energy. In 1932 the National Government swept Free Trade into limbo at the Ottawa Conference; henceforth our industrial and financial energies, instead of being dissipated over the whole globe, were to be concentrated to produce a more stable economy in our own Commonwealth, and the states most closely allied to it. There was a steady increase in prosperity, and London became once more the financial centre of the Dominions. The new imperial self-consciousness became evident in the activities of a host of voluntary associations—Imperial Institutes, Bureaux and Committees for various kinds of scientific research, Imperial Press and Parliamentary Conferences, and many others. The Dominions were associated with the administration of the Colonial Empire. At the Imperial Conference of 1930 the Dominions were mainly interested in increased autonomy; at that of 1937 in increased co-operation. Already, the mere threat of war had begun the work of regeneration.

[1] Albert Viton, *Great Britain*, 100-1.

§3

Then the countries already visibly on the verge of that complete self-government within the Commonwealth which just now is called Dominion status; and in particular, India, with a population of more than two hundred and fifty millions. Nobody planned the conquest of India. India was not conquered, and is not held, by the sword. As elsewhere, British merchants went to trade, and having set up trading stations, found themselves compelled to preserve order. British rule was extended gradually and, for the most part, reluctantly. It has given India much which India would not have had without it, and in the first place, itself; for there was no "India" before the British went there, only a subcontinent of warring nations. In addition, internal peace, Western science, the Rule of Law, and a century and a half of splendidly uncorrupt administration. Acts as far back as 1833 prohibited a colour bar for any public office; since 1861 Indians have been entering the Indian Civil Service in free competition with Englishmen. The British Parliament knew well enough what it was doing when, as far back as 1853, it decided to give Indians the education of the West, with its constant emphasis on liberty. As Macaulay put it, "I will never consent to keep them ignorant in order to keep them manageable or to govern them in ignorance in order that we may govern them long." With whatever mistakes, India has long been governed with the avowed object that she should one day govern herself. That, at least, is no mean ideal. And for some while India has at any rate been free enough to use her own tariff to shut out more than £50,000,000 worth of British goods, and Lancashire

225

operatives have gone idle that the Indian cotton trade might boom. In a century and a half, for good or ill, India has passed from a medley of warring mediæval princedoms to a modern nation about to take its equal place, with Canada and Australia, in a great Commonwealth of free, white peoples. This in itself is one of the great achievements of history. Nor is it surprising that while she has been approaching the threshold of freedom, the impatience of vocal India should have increased. Politically and administratively the British have succeeded. Culturally and socially they have failed. Business, administration and big-game shooting, these have been our real contacts with India; in literature, art and society there are none. Not a dozen men in Britain know anything of the work of the younger Indian poets and novelists. British society in India lives spiritually entrenched in an invisible Aldershot, or an impalpable suburbia, beyond which the varied, brightly coloured life of the Indian millions is as remote as if lived upon another hemisphere. One of the most influential Indian Nationalists of to-day was educated at a famous English public school, and left it with many English friends, and devoted to England and its ways; to this day a photograph of the school cricket team hangs upon his wall. He went back to India to find that insolent British merchants treated him as "a native." Since then he has been a passionate advocate of complete independence for India. Again, of purposeful economic development, of effective social services India has not seen much under British rule. All-pervasive poverty, a high mortality rate, vast illiteracy, primitive agriculture, these familiar features of an oriental society may to some extent, though only to some extent, be laid at the door of British administration. (And let those who are tempted to overstress the social backwardness of India under British rule compare its present condition with that of Afghanistan, whose potential wealth per head is much greater, and whose population has always been more vigorous than that of India.) And it is probable that the training for self-government, which we have indisputably bestowed on India, alone and of itself outweighs all these short-comings. For those who mistrust the ancient British instinct that liberty is the indispensable basis of all public virtues would do well to observe its rapid effects in countries such as Egypt and India. At home so many generations have been brought up to liberty that its moral consequences are taken for granted as part of our national heredity. But in Egypt or India it is possible to study the effects of the impact of freedom upon an unfree society. Mr. Albert Viton, an American who is a most hostile critic of our social record in India, writes as follows:

"Or compare India with Java. Which of the two has had the smoother and more efficient administration cannot be doubted: Java's social services have been much better than those provided by the British for India. Yet the former is almost as far from self-determination as it has ever been, while India has not only had a very vigorous political movement but has demonstrated its ability to lead an almost completely independent life. . . . While Java's moral fibre has strengthened hardly at all during the past centuries, or to a degree that is almost negligible, that of India has grown in a manner that is nothing short of amazing. In 1882 Seeley feared that 'the few facts we know about the ancient Hindus confirm what we should conjecture about the moral effects produced on them' by foreign rule. We know now that British rule has not only not had disastrous results, but has perhaps done 'more than ever was done by former Governments to make . . . possible' for India to 'begin to breathe as a single national whole.' " [1]

If two hundred and fifty million Indians had really wished to get rid of sixty thousand British soldiers and six thousand British civil servants, they would not have found the task impossible. And what would despotism on the Nazi model have made of India by now—a huge, servile prison-camp, terrorised by the secret police, and bristling with barracks and munition-factories? Vast achievements and melancholy failures—of such is our record in India. But history will, I think, reckon the achievements more prodigious than the failures. And here, too, the threat of the totalitarians, and then the coming of war, have begun to work as a leaven. Even the Indian who resents British supremacy most bitterly is reminded that British rule has stood between him and something infinitely baser and more humiliating. Industrial production in India will be rapidly modernised and developed in the stress of war, and Indians will be much more readily admitted to responsibility in the various services. And in Britain, behind the scenes, a handful of clear-sighted and influential men is working to establish that broader intellectual understanding between the two peoples without which political ties must be empty forms.

[1] Albert Viton, *Great Britain*, 62.

§4

The Dependencies—Crown Colonies, Protectorates and mandated territories. Nearly two million square miles, and nearly fifty million human beings. Here, too, there has been extraordinarily little blood shed. In Africa, often treated as the scene of acquisitive imperialism at its worst, as in India, British Governments have extended their rule with surprising reluctance. Once the machine had come to Europe, Europeans began to need first the raw materials of Africa and then the African market for manufactured goods; wherever Britain did not go, some other European country would have taken control. This was the chief motive for British expansion in Africa. It was not entirely selfish. Cecil Rhodes, who was long thought of as the personification of acquisitive imperialism, believed passionately in an equalitarian, non-militarist Empire; the more British rule, the better for the world at large, and the better for the Africans, who would at last be freed from the endless disorder and destruction of slave-raiding and slave-trading. It stands to reason that some of the picture is dark: it is mainly of the nineteenth century that we are speaking, and it was not to be expected that its greedy materialism should be confined to the home country. Moreover modern agriculture and irrigation, up-to-date social services, a systematic development of natural resources would be even harder to point to in the Colonies than in India. Here and there land settlement has been glaringly unjust to the native. Even so, the darkness can easily be exaggerated. Sierra Leone was not expressing its own sentiments only when it sent a gift to Great Britain lately "in grateful recognition of the great benefits which Sierra Leone has received during the last 135 years under the British Flag." And one needs only to compare the social advances in, say, Tanganyika or Fiji with the primitive immobility of Abyssinia or Thibet to realise what British rule has in fact accomplished, even where it has been most backward. Nor is it possible to overlook either the competence or the idealism which pervades the story. As a most astringent critic of our colonial performance has put it:

"The fact is that countries like Iraq, Turkey, Iran, and various Baltic states have discovered after experimenting with officials and experts from all over the world that the British give far more devoted and disinterested and useful service." [1]

Two of the greatest and yet most typical figures in the history of British Africa are Wilberforce and Livingstone; the Evangelical statesman who devoted his life to abolishing the slave trade, and the missionary whose devotion to the Africans was as unbounded as his prestige in Britain, and whose formula for civilising Africa was Christianity, commerce and colonisation. The doctrine of imperial trusteeship, developed in Africa during the last twenty years, is the same principle which elsewhere in the Commonwealth has created responsible self-government, modified here to suit primitive conditions. It has led the Government to lay down the guiding maxim that wherever the interests of natives and Europeans conflict, native interests must be preferred. "H.M. Government regard themselves as exercising a trust on behalf of the native population . . . the object of which may be defined as the protection and

[1] Albert Viton, *Great Britain*, 326.

advancement of the native races:" so ran an official declaration of policy in 1923. What sort of trust? And what sort of advancement—for without the definition of a goal "advancement" is as meaningless as "progress"? In practice the principle of trusteeship has implied, firstly, Indirect Rule; rule, that is, through native chiefs, or chiefs-in-council, the natural trustees of African tradition; a training for Africans in administration, justice and even law-making within their own African background.

"The chiefs of Kilimanjaro, who for centuries and until the establishment of European rule made ceaseless warfare on each other and who five years ago would scarcely meet, are now grouped in three Councils, each of which has a common treasury and is constituted as a court of appeal. . . ." [1]

And secondly, "trusteeship" has meant abandoning the French method, which was originally the British method, too, of educating Africans in European traditions, social habits and culture. Instead of turning the African into a superficial imitation of a fourth-rate European, education was to help him to be a better African. Let him assimilate the best of what Europe has to offer, but remain rooted in African soil. Clearly at the best of times a prodigious problem of adjustment, and with Europe itself critically sick from the accumulated poisons of a century of materialism, a task, one might be tempted to suppose, almost too great for human powers. And yet —all this can by now be seen to represent only the beginnings, under startlingly different conditions, of

[1] *Report to the Council of the League of Nations on the Administration of Tanganyika for 1927*, 98.

the same process as that now completed in the Dominions, and nearing its completion in India, a collective journey towards the distant goal of a Commonwealth consisting of nothing but "autonomous communities . . ., equal in status . . . united by a common allegiance to the Crown."

"Over the vast field as a whole there seems to be no intrinsic reason why it should not go on smoothly to its end. A Dominion of Nigeria for example? Why not?" [1]

And meanwhile the very definition of such a goal, and the movement towards it, in its appropriate atmosphere of respect for human individuality and civil rights, possesses a sanitary moral property of its own, disinfecting and compensating for many failures in other fields. Compare, for example, Syria, ruled by the French since 1920, with Egypt. In 1914 Syria was economically, culturally and politically far ahead of Egypt. Syria's newspapers were the best in the Near East, its literature the most vigorous; the whole Arab world drew upon its intelligentsia for teachers, doctors, merchants and officials. Since 1920 there has been a steady regression. Egypt, and even Iraq, both countries once controlled by Britain but given complete independence, have passed it long since.

"That the differences between British and other imperial rules should add up to such imposing totals may be surprising. However, history shows that they do. The results are seen throughout the colonial world, regardless which colonies one will compare.

[1] Professor Coupland, *The Empire in these Days*, 179.

Even the British possessions in Africa, more neglected than all others, compare favourably with those of France, Portugal or Italy; and the differences will become even greater in subsequent years, when the British colonies will be better prepared to make use of their greater freedom." [1]

Despite backwardness and complacency, oversights and selfishness, the fact remains that the principle of growth is incorporated in the very vitals of the British Commonwealth. And growth is all. This in itself is one of the great achievements of history.

And in the Colonial Dependencies, too, the threat of the totalitarians after 1935 produced a new outbreak of energy in just those fields in which our administration had been most backward. Education, health, child welfare, agriculture, nutrition and land-settlement—all these problems were freshly studied and attacked. Organised campaigns against soil-erosion in Tanganyika or Ceylon and sleeping-sickness in Nigeria, pasture improvements in Mauritius or the Falkland Islands, small-holdings in Jamaica, new education departments in Aden or Somaliland, more education, new labour and trade union legislation and industrial welfare regulations; such were a few of the consequences. Natives of the colonies are to be admitted to administrative posts hitherto closed to them. The headmaster of a famous English public school left to become Principal of an East African College. Many native schools for nurses, midwives and sanitary workers were opened. Once again the Empire was changing. Here, too, the mere threat of war had brought regeneration.

[1] Albert Viton, *Great Britain*, 62.

§ 5

This world-wide, immensely varied and constantly developing system, so frequently to all appearances on the verge of dissolution, yet so regularly and so surprisingly surviving, has meant permanent domestic peace for more than a quarter of the world's population, over a quarter of the world's surface. And since armed conflict between the British Commonwealth and the United States has become unthinkable, not far short of half the world may be said to have already entered the fabled age when wars shall be no more. The British Commonwealth is a League of Nations which worked. Moreover, it gave mankind from 1815 to 1914 the first century without a major war since the break-up of the Roman Empire. A world currency based on gold, free trade and free immigration all helped to maintain peace, but the prime agent was a paramount British Navy; there could be no world war until there arose, in Germany, a power capable of challenging Great Britain at sea. A navy, it will be observed, can maintain the peace, but it cannot become an instrument of tyranny. And the British Commonwealth has been the least military of all imperial systems known to history. Before the outbreak of the present war the Dominions had come nearer to complete disarmament than any modern state except Luxemburg, and the total military strength of the sixty-odd colonies was less than thirty thousand men, most of whom were in semi-police organisations. It is easy to overlook the social and economic advantages to the Dominions, to India and to the Colonies of protection by the British Navy, supported by the British taxpayer. But for the Navy Australia and New Zealand would not have been able to spend their time and their money on constructive social experiments. All the direct and indirect contributions of the Dominions, India and the Colonies to all the wars of the Empire represent but a fraction of what they would have had to spend if they had been outside the Commonwealth. The Navy has made the British Commonwealth a profoundly unmilitary society—a society in fact which has been steadily relinquishing precisely that old-fashioned type of imperial power which the totalitarians are seeking to re-establish.

The British Commonwealth is a phenomenon to which history affords no parallel. It is not surprising, therefore, that even well-informed and intelligent foreigners should be childishly ignorant of its nature; so that cultured Americans can believe that the "open spaces" of the Dominions are available for any British citizen who chooses to emigrate, or that Great Britain "owns" Australia. What is much more surprising, and much more discreditable, is that countless British citizens are equally ill-informed—so that to-day there is even said to be a danger that Dominion troops stationed in this island may be antagonised by the unexpected ignorance and indifference of their hosts as to Commonwealth affairs. In part political influences have been responsible for their ignorance. Particularly among Socialists and Liberals there has long been a tradition, of the kind which is accepted without reflection as an article of faith, that anything associated with the word Empire must be discreditable—for Socialists largely because Empire suggests exploiting capitalism, for Liberals largely because is suggests aggressive militarism. On these curiously inadequate grounds Socialists have turned their backs on the widest opportunities for state planning and beneficent social service ever offered to any people in any age, and

Liberals have shut their eyes to the greatest effort to promote human liberty yet known to history. The vastest political, economic and social problems and opportunities which statesmen have ever been confronted with, and perhaps seven politicians out of ten are more interested in Sunday cinemas or the dole. What the Colonial Empire " is for, apart from the material power it embodies, it would not be so easy to explain," writes the Socialist Professor Laski,[1] but not a few Socialist lecturers have toured North America to explain that what in effect it "is for" is to enrich a few capitalists, and to obstruct "the forces of progress." I was present myself, shortly before the outbreak of this war, at a discussion in an undergraduates' club in which every speaker treated the British Commonwealth as immoral or outmoded. In so far as the indifference or hostility of so many British citizens towards the greatest political achievement of their own, or any, race is no more than a reaction against the self-conscious, acquisitive imperialism of the last generation or two, and still more if it represents a survival of the ancient humanitarian tradition in our public life, it may be said to have played a most valuable part, as a sort of disinfectant of imperial policy, filling more or less the rôle of a permanently critical and observant Opposition. But in so far as hostility, or apathy, has been founded on sheer ignorance it is difficult not to regard it as a symptom of decadence. The citizens of Rôme in the age of the Antonines doubtless had a shrewd idea of what Rome stood for, and there is no evidence that it caused them either shame or irritation. But our ignorance is by no means only due to politics. British schools do not teach the history of the British Commonwealth of Nations. For better or for worse, to put it at its lowest,

[1] *Political Quarterly*, October-December, 1938.

the growth of the British Commonwealth has made us what we are; in the darkest hour of civilisation the British Commonwealth stood alone between mankind and the new barbarism; if we survive this war, the future of the world manifestly will depend upon the British Commonwealth—and yet we do not teach its history in our schools. We teach the history of the War of the Austrian Succession, dead, remote and long since meaningless—but we do not teach the history of the British Commonwealth. Last year, of nine Boards which examine for the School Certificate, only four set a paper on imperial history, and these four papers were taken by only 850 candidates out of the 23,800 who offered History as a subject. As for the Oxford and Cambridge Joint Board, it set a special paper on the making of the German Empire, but none on the making of the British Empire. None of the nine Boards set a compulsory question on imperial history in its general history paper. In the Higher Certificate examination no Board sets History candidates a paper on imperial history. In some examinations imperial history figures as one of a number of optional subjects—in 1939 about four per cent of the Oxford and Cambridge Joint Board's History candidates chose a paper on " Colonial" History— and in some general history papers there will be an optional question on the Commonwealth, for the most part discreetly avoided by the examinees, whose instructors have not failed to recognise that their charges can obtain their Certificates without it. As for the Universities, it is possible to be placed in the First Class in the School of Modern History at either Oxford or Cambridge without knowing any imperial history whatever. And so, while modern-minded men like Mr. Lionel Curtis or the late Lord Lothian spent their lives upon the

vast world-problems of this steadily evolving association
of one-quarter of the human race, many a politician
proudly counting himself "progressive" was scarcely so
much as aware that such problems existed, or supposed
that a conventional sneer or two at some defunct Victorian slogan about white men's burdens, or painting the
map red, finally qualified him as an authoritative critic
of empire.

There is a vicious circle in all this. The politician is
ignorant or apathetic because the schoolboy is not taught,
and the schoolboy is not taught because the politician is
ignorant or apathetic. And because the politician is
ignorant or apathetic, social services in the Colonies have
come too slowly, and Czechoslovakia has been apt to
rouse more interest at Westminster than Canada. And
emigration has died away. There was a great opportunity for the development and settlement of the
Dominions after the last war, but, with many other
opportunities about that time, we wasted it. The Empire
Settlement Act of 1922, and all the Dominion statutes
which went with it, is dead—killed by the hostility of
organised labour overseas, reluctant to share its advantages, by the opposition of the Dutch in South Africa, and
the indifference of the French Canadians.

§ 6

Much that has been said goes to suggest that immediately after the war, if we survive the war, there may
first follow a phase of serious strain in our imperial
relations. Even if, this time, there is no widespread
cultural reaction against the war itself, the men who
fought it and the system out of which it grew, there will

nevertheless be the young war industries in the Dominions, which they may wish to protect with a tariff of their own, while to some it will begin to seem that the protection of the Royal Navy is no longer required. In the Colonies, moreover, feeling against British rule will no longer be damped down by the fear of the dark alternative of Fascism. And in India war-industrialisation will have greatly enlarged that middle class which no oriental society knew before its contact with the West, and which everywhere and always has been your only begetter of revolutions. But if we are able to survive the war, it will be because we are fit to survive, and because we are *meant* to survive, and we shall certainly contrive to weather the post-war reaction. Indeed, the future of the British Commonwealth, once it has survived the war, must be splendid indeed. Its prestige and influence, as the power which saved mankind, will be unparalleled. More than ever before it will be the unconscious schoolmaster of the world. But the great rôle to be played in a new age will mean, once again, far-reaching changes and re-orientations.

Mere British patriotism, the Anglo-Saxon race fanaticism of Cecil Rhodes, will not be sufficient to hold the vast structure together. British racial patriotism will remain, a fundamental and energising force, but it will be merged in a wider conception, clearly implicit in the dreams of Rhodes, the conception of community of civilisation. The bond uniting a Commonwealth of so many colours, creeds and races, will be the British conception of a national life founded upon the ideals of tolerance, personal liberty and the Rule of Law. Not colour, race or creed, but the extent to which these ideals have taken root, will be the measure of political maturity. India will forthwith be admitted to full equality in the Commonwealth, and will be followed by Burma, Ceylon, Jamaica, Bermuda and other members in steady succession. The age-old problem of the relations of East and West will have been transformed. But in the last resort the survival and vitality of the Commonwealth will depend, in the future as in the past, on the services which it renders to its members, and to the world. It will not disappear until some other social organisation displaces it by rendering the same services more cheaply, more reliably or more unselfishly. The services which the Commonwealth will render to its members will alter, no doubt, in character, but fundamentally they will remain the same which it has rendered in the past. First and foremost, there is defence, that world-wide protection by the British Navy which has enabled so many communities to combine the social structure of a highly civilised state with the military establishment of a tenth-rate power. The military power of the Commonwealth at the end of a victorious war will be immensely greater than it was at the beginning. In conjunction, it is to be hoped, with the United States and Russia, it is bound for some while to police the world. It is not likely, with the melancholy consequences of disarmament after the last war fresh in our minds, either that we shall throw our weapons away as soon as the war is over, or that the members of the Commonwealth will be in a hurry to dispense with its protection. Secondly, the Commonwealth has had the advantage of remarkable financial services. In 1911 India was able to borrow at $3\frac{1}{2}$ per cent, whereas, outside the Commonwealth, to judge from the example of Japan, she would have had to pay at least $5\frac{1}{2}$ per cent. The London market has supplied members of the Commonwealth with the funds needed for development, without their having to beg, like independent countries, from one capital to another; their political connection, too, has enabled them to carry through funding operations which have saved them millions of pounds a year. After the war imperial banking and currency are likely to be reorganised on a more unitary system, and Britain may decide to pay for war purchases by floating loans in the Dominions, which will make them for the first time her creditors—a natural development likely to be welcome overseas. Thirdly, in the Dependencies, there has been British administration. As we have seen, British administration has had its notable faults, but it can hardly be disputed that it has been more uncorrupt, more lenient and, on the whole, more acceptable to native populations than that of any other imperial power known to history. That it has brought great social advances can be seen by comparing Tanganyika with Thibet; that it has been efficient, by contrasting the British irrigation system in Egypt with the dams built before 1882 with foreign aid, ten times as expensive and ten times less effective; that it has been welcome, by noting that, after Egypt and Iraq had become completely independent, and able to choose what administration they pleased, they did not dismiss their British officials. It has been fashionable of late with a number of literary and academic intellectuals at home to decry British rule in the Colonies, the principal charge being that it has been unimaginative and unsympathetic. Unlike Egypt and Iraq, many of these domestic critics preferred Russian officials, at a distance at any rate, to their own fellow-countrymen. This is not a verdict which the world at large endorses. In the new age British officials will have increasingly to co-operate with reformers and nationalists in countries well on the way to complete self-government. For this, their record, not only within the

Commonwealth but outside it, has shown them to be admirably qualified. Mr. Albert Viton has plenty of hard things to say of our colonial administration, but he concludes:

> "The fact is that countries like Iraq, Turkey, Iran and various Baltic states have discovered after experimenting with officials and experts from all over the world that the British give far more devoted and disinterested and useful service. A British expert in, say, the new Turkish Government would not think of informing his ambassador of what is taking place inside government offices; the same cannot be said about other European nationals." [1]

The qualities and defects of British administration combine to make it uniquely fitted to play a creative part in a new age of developing self-government.

§7

In what kind of world will it be possible for the British Commonwealth to play such a rôle? In a world in which, for as far ahead as we can at present hope to see, the Commonwealth and the United States, in alliance, let us hope, with Russia, share paramount power and influence. The British Commonwealth and the United States— these are the two systems which, for all their faults, have genuinely believed in freedom. They have developed the vices as well as the virtues of freedom, but if they survive this war, they will have proved that their vices were not mortal. These are the only two great powers whose

[1] Albert Viton, *Great Britain*, 326.

supremacy we can conceive of as permitting other nations to develop their own individualities. Their closest co-operation will be needed to see the world through that period after the war during which its new spiritual and political contours will begin to take shape. "What an awful thought it is that if we had not lost America, or if even now we could arrange with the present members of the United States Assembly and our House of Commons, the peace of the world is secured for all eternity," wrote Cecil Rhodes in 1891. Since then two world wars have underlined the lesson that without Anglo-American co-operation there cannot be peace. These two systems possess a common speech which is the mother-tongue of two hundred millions, and the second language of most of the rest of the world; as well as a literature which, from King James' Bible to the *Elegy in a Country Church-yard*, belongs to both, and since then has been shared between them. Canada is the hyphen between the two systems: Canada which is both British and American, Canada whose frontier with the United States has been undefended for a hundred years. At this point some will exclaim, "Federal Union." I am not looking so far ahead. For the more immediate future it is sufficient that close co-operation between the United States and ourselves will inevitably act as a magnet upon all those countries which share the ideals of liberty, tolerance and the Rule of Law. The idea of Federal Union, with its core of no less than fifteen "founder democracies," was born in the last desperate years of the old regime, when peace was dying swiftly and men were minded to clutch at any straw before they drowned. But after this war there will be peace for many years; for either the dictators or the great democracies will police the world. No need now to act precipitately. Federal Union may come, but there will be time for it to grow, like all political systems which have endured. No need for it to spring ready-armed, like Minerva from the brow of Jove, or the League of Nations from that of President Wilson. Time for some of the fifteen prospective founder democracies to purge themselves of their Quislings, or meditate upon the merits of neutrality. Time for the two real founder democracies to explore and cement the fuller possibilities of their own working alliance. But that at some time some form of wider union must come, with the British Commonwealth as its core, seems to lie in the logic of history. Nor is there lacking evidence that already the smaller western democracies are turning their eyes in this direction—a speech, for example, by the Foreign Minister of Norway, Herr Trygve Lie, in December of 1940. This would no longer be the British Commonwealth, but a world system into which it would be the historic mission of the Commonwealth to carry its own traditions of liberty, tolerance and the Rule of Law, and of change without violence. It may be that such a system would coalesce, not through any deliberate framing of a complete federal structure, but through the gradual admission of citizens of all its constituent nations to its administrative service. In two hundred years Indians have first become a new nation, which did not exist before their contact with the British, and then learned themselves increasingly to rule it. It will not be two hundred years before there are Indian administrators outside India. Without such a wider system, the most fundamental, most insistent of all problems of mankind must remain unsolved—How shall wars be prevented? For no police force alone, whether that of a few dominant powers or of some supreme world organisation, can permanently keep the peace for mankind. In the world, as in the nation, peace cannot rest upon force alone; there must be justice. And justice between nations means some still undiscovered alternative to the crucible of war as a means of testing the fitness of peoples, systems and ideas to survive, and of their rivals to supplant them. In a world society whose huge central core was the British Commonwealth, the vital principle of which has been peaceful growth and change, it is most likely that an ascendant race-strain would be able to assert its superiority without violence, providing an increasing proportion of the administrators, the teachers, the political and indus-trial leaders of the vast community. This, and not a paper charter, or even an international police force, would be the beginning of world peace. Hitherto in world history a society which has reached political maturity has always sooner or later been crushed by the rise of a new power, proudly aware of its virility, and convinced that the might, of which it is so conscious, must be right. And so the vicious circle is complete. To break that vicious circle, the society which has reached political maturity will have to take a further step for-ward, and, like all morally creative actions, that step forward must be a form of self-surrender. The Un-official Conference on British Commonwealth relations held at Sydney in 1938 agreed that if the Commonwealth was to continue to perform a worthy function, it must become "a dynamic Commonwealth," deriving inspira-tion from something outside itself. Undoubtedly that something is the Christian precept to consider the in-terests of a neighbour as of equal importance with one's own. A counsel of perfection it may seem, for when has a statesman yet opposed some course which was obviously to the advantage of his own people, because it would be obviously harmful to another nation? Yet such is the step forward which destiny will soon demand of us. It will mean a sublimation of the dream of Joseph Chamberlain and Cecil Rhodes, of world peace through the extension of the Pax Britannica into every corner of the earth. The Pax Britannica will be extended indeed, not by direct British rule, but by the influence of the British Commonwealth as the core of a new world society.

> "If . . . we are too small-minded, if we lack the courage and the humility to impregnate politics with religion, then we shall drift apart into our petty and respective nationalisms: and we and the world in general will be the poorer for it. If so, primitive imperialism will stalk the earth in triumph again, and the human race will have to wait long years for the slow process of sublimation to be repeated before it can again assay to bridge the chasm to a world order. But if we succeed, even if only in part, the British Commonwealth will then surrender its identity in a wider organism, its contribution made, and its existence in history justified." [1]

§8

The League of Nations? For as soon as the last bomb has fallen, amiable and benevolent ideologues, we may be sure, will be waiting letter-perfect with the draft of a new League, differing (to judge from some of their recent publications) only in the most insignificant details from the contraption which had perished of its own rigidity, half-heartedness and excessive assumptions, long before

[1] Professor Vincent Harlow, *The Character of British Imperialism*, 37-8.

246

the final challenge sounded and the uncovenanted members of the British Commonwealth rose to meet it. Let the League, like the Commonwealth, like the United States, and like the new world society which will one day coalesce about these two, be content with modest beginnings. As a voluntary agent for international discussion, and arbitration, as a clearing-house for economic and scientific research, as a centre of international social services, there is plenty for it to do. But at first it will be the work of scientists, lawyers and philosophers, not of statesmen or soldiers. Let it begin here. And if the vital spark is in it, it will grow. If the vital spark is in it, it may even one day outgrow the Anglo-American alliance, and whatever peoples have rallied to it, assume political and even military functions, and become at last in truth the organisation universal. But that day is assuredly not yet, and paper plans which assume that it is, can only once again postpone it indefinitely, once again at the cost, may be, of much blood and tears. And meanwhile may we remember that no institution can be nobler than its membership, and be spared a repetition of the ironic spectacle of worthy, but uninstructed, British citizens (for many of whom their own Government could do nothing right) proclaiming the tortuous intrigues of Balkan politicians to be the very embodiment of religion in politics, for the simple reason that they were spun in the corridors of Geneva. Growth is all. For all we can yet tell, there may be the greatest of futures before the League; but only if it takes the growth of the tree, and not the assembling of the machine, for its model. New and complex economic machinery, a new conception of trade, effective international regulation of immigration, nationality, currency, labour, shipping, air transport, and a host of other matters, a vast new civil service and a world navy, army, and air force, the uprooting of many old loyalties and a world-wide cultural revolution—all this, at the least, will have to be effected if the League is indeed to become the paramount world organisation. It may be that one day all this will indeed come to pass, but if it does, it will be because the Anglo-American association has shown the world the way. And meanwhile there is the British Commonwealth, a quarter of the world in a League of Nations which works.

VIII

CONCLUSION

WE shall not win this war because one day we may have better weapons than the enemy, but because we are more worthy to survive than he is—of which our having better weapons may one day be a symptom. Weighed thus in the scales of history, we shall be wise to spend less time on proclaiming the shortcomings of the enemy— on which we may rest assured that the Shaper of destinies is entirely competent to pronounce—than on meditating, and amending, our own. In the mood of to-day penitence, surely, should be mingled with faith, resolution and defiance. In the days of old, when Israel was threatened with destruction, it was the false prophets who pro- phesied comfortable things, but the true prophets who summoned the people to sackcloth and ashes. And if there were true prophets to-day, would they not be bidding us to remember our sins, and repent them, instead of assuring us (as the Planners of New Orders so often seem to do) that the true meaning of the war is that we are soon to have a better time than ever. It is easier for the false prophets to-day than in ages when the existence of God was more widely known, and most men had some inkling of the spiritual consequences of suffer- ing. Yet is there not danger as well as blindness in popularising the notion that it needs a war to make us really comfortable?

Some such considerations as these must be my excuse if I have offered few suggestions as to how we are to make ourselves more comfortable after the war, or have seemed to have too much to say of what we have done amiss, and too little of what we have done well. Looking back, it is not difficult to see that all our failures spring from the same root, an age of materialism. It was materialism which led us to mistake increasing comfort for progress, and materialism, elated by the rapid triumphs of science, which persuaded us to overrate the capacities of pure intellect, divorced from every other human quality; with the twofold result that the goal of the "progress" which we worshipped proves to be catastrophe, and that many of those who led us towards it have been men without judgment or courage. And so, since materialism is the root of all our troubles, it follows that the change which is at once most necessary and most radical is that we should cease to be materialists. This is our great, last opportunity, the opportunity offered to men at all the great turning-points of history, the opportunity of regeneration through suffering. This is the inmost meaning of the war; the opportunity of that victory over ourselves without which we shall not be worthy to survive, or shape a new age. This is the hardest of all our tasks, for it is not the reform of others, but of ourselves; not the suppression of other people's privileges, but the surrender of our own; not the laying of burdens on our neighbours, but the conquest of the greedy coward in our own hearts; not the drafting of paper constitutions, but a deadly wrestling with our own selves. As always, suffering was needed, if there was to be regeneration, suffering which shatters illusion, by forcing us to recognise that evil, in the form of pain, is unmistakably present in our own existence; forcing on our unwilling attention the need to adjust ourselves to the real universe; making it easy at last to abandon the way of life which we would not surrender so long as it was still agreeable.

Conclusion

Some of such reforms as have been suggested in these pages have been intended as an assault upon the root evil itself, blind and greedy materialism. Others have been concerned with each of the two main branches which spring from that root, the illusion that the goal of man is a higher standard of living (to which Christians so often seem to subscribe), and the illusion of the sufficiency of the pure intellect, divorced from sound character, practical experience and spiritual insight.

For myself, if we survive the war I do not foresee the enforcement of any of those comprehensive -isms from which their various devotees expect a cure for all the ills of society. As for Socialism, it is strange to hear its mystics still discussing it in the future tense, for already, to-day, the state possesses far greater power over the individual than most of the Socialist prophets ever dreamed of, or the British are ever likely to tolerate in peace-time. Genuine all-embracing Socialism, the Socialism which means the subjection of *every* private interest to the state, we are scarcely likely to see; for it is impossible now to imagine circumstances which would induce British Socialists who could oppose Conscription in 1939 and wage stabilisation in 1941, even to desire, much less to construct, a genuinely Socialist society. We shall doubtless make considerable advances towards the completely Collectivist State, and the conditions of 1949 will in many ways be more like what we are accustomed to think of as Socialism than were those of 1939. But then the conditions of 1939 would themselves have seemed pure Socialism to any one who could have foreseen them in 1914. And underlying our Collectivism in the future, as in the past, will be that ineradicable strain of individualism in our heredity which softens the asperities, and contradicts the logic, of the

System. I know of no evidence, for example, that complete economic equalitarianism of the kind which some deduce from the Socialist premises, would be acceptable to any but the most insignificant minority of our people. It could only claim authority from the New Testament, if it implied a deliberate and universal acceptance of absolute poverty, and would only be logical if it aimed, as it does not, at the economic equality of all men, of whatever race or colour, everywhere.

What I hope to see is a nation traditionalist, in that it is not afraid to carry into the new age the creative traditions of the past, revolutionary in that, where the experience of these terrible years has shown that there is dead wood to be cut out, it allows no tradition to tamper it, not even the revolutionary tradition. I hope for a democracy which, for the present at any rate, when it says Progress, will mean better citizens, and not more comfort. And this is why more revolutionary changes are needed in education than in any other department of state. For the first time in our history, education must be education of men, not of intelligences only, a comprehensive training in spirit, mind, body and character. If we are wise, the public schools—for the first time, their economic exclusiveness broken down, fully justifying their name—will furnish, from the traditions of the older England, the basis on which the new Britain may build the wider education of the future. When the new comprehensive schooling has compelled the examination system to foster and search, not for intelligence only, but for intelligence rounded and reinforced by all the other qualities which make for achievement, the English may even begin, for the first time in their history, to be genuinely interested in education. The schools, I hope, will do even more than economics to transform and obliterate class barriers. But they will achieve none of these purposes for long if they do not recover a Christian background. Out of no other strand in the texture of our heredity can come that consciousness of Ends which must supersede our obsession with Means. Since our history is what it is, only Christianity can save us from the civilisation of the cinema, the road house, and the radio set. Whether it will indeed, one distant day, so save us, we shall know soon, for unless we become fit for something better in the course of our present ordeal, we shall not survive it.

Seen against this background of gradual escape from the bleak inferno of materialism, the changes which have seemed to me likely and desirable in industry fulfil a two-fold purpose. They turn the irritating futility of work, which may mean only earning wages, into the humane dignity of public service. But I hope that they will do more than this, and that we may learn to maintain in peace the standards to which hitherto we have only risen in war, and habitually honour service of whatever kind above profit-making on whatever scale. With vast incomes no longer to be made, and industry increasingly a field for public service rather than fortune-hunting, society may even gradually relearn the Christian scale of values, and give the saint, the hero, the thinker and the artist their proper due. But the reform of industry must in a real sense be secondary to the reform of ourselves, since any system whatever controlled by disinterested Christians will be preferable to any system whatever controlled by self-seeking atheists.

There will be many attempts to "capture" the war for other purposes. For Russia, for example—with the suggestion that the Russian system has at one and the same time been not really so different from our own, and also very much better. Poignantly aware of the gallantry and sufferings of the Russians, and of the magnitude of some of their social achievements, it may be difficult for us to remember that Russia, too, has been a materialist totalitarian state, which cared little that democracy seemed upon the verge of destruction, and that it is possible for us to be the allies and well-wishers of a despot, as we were in 1814 and 1914, without admiring despotism. Or the war may be "captured" for a materialist's New Social Order—ever the line of least resistance. Or, for that matter, for Big Business, or Temperance or Bureaucracy, or Militarism. But all these are irrelevant to the true meaning of the war. It is for national regeneration, moral and spiritual, that we must look now, if we would survive.

THE END